AND THE *Birds* STILL *Sing*

SUE SHRYOCK FRALEY

ISBN 979-8-88616-930-0 (paperback)
ISBN 979-8-88616-931-7 (digital)

Christian Faith Publishing
832 Park Avenue
Meadville, PA 16335
www.christianfaithpublishing.com

Printed in the United States of America

To my Lord and Savior, Jesus Christ. Without you, this book would have been an impossible task; but with you, I am learning that all things are possible. Thank you, Lord, for showing me I can!

In Psalm 45:1, "My heart overflows with a good theme; I address my Psalm to the King. My tongue is like the pen of a skillful writer."

The Choir

Through the fire, through the rain
Through the trials, through the pain
I hear the choir without fail.
They gather together before the dawn
They praise you with their continuous song
With no audience, they joyfully sing
In beautiful harmony, they praise their king
I hear the choir without fail.
Never do they cease to meet
With one accord they are complete
A powerful witness to the listening ear
Who stops to listen, who stops to hear?
Yes! Listen to these little ones
Every morning as they come
I hear the choir without fail.
No matter what the weather brings
God has taught me that the birds still sing!

Crossover

Mom, I didn't see you cross over, no, I wasn't there.
Words left unspoken that I wanted to share
My heart aches, but the memories are sweet
I know that you're worshiping at our Savior's feet
Although I miss you, I wouldn't change one thing
I'm reminded of where you are, each time I hear the birds sing!

I love you, Mom!

In loving memory of Regenia Mae Shryock
1940–2005

Contents

Introduction

I want to invite you into my journey, one that I'm confident many can relate to on multiple levels. This book that you are about to read was born out of the will of God despite my moments of "I can't do this, Lord." During one of my doubting moments, the Lord spoke to me and said, "Stop saying, 'I can't.' You are hindering the work I want to do through you. Stand before me as a willing vessel ready to receive." With that being said and being divinely inspired, I moved forward with what you now hold in your hands.

Written within the pages of this book are tragedy, heartache, rebellion, and brokenness; but you will find divine appointments, miracles, and triumph as well. As you take part in my journey, I pray that you come away knowing with confidence that God is faithful; God is a healer; God is loving; and God is trustworthy, merciful, and forever constant. Though our journey in life can, at times, be painful and tumultuous, we can be assured of triumphant victory if we continue to follow God's perfect plan.

In 1 Corinthians 15:57, "But thanks be to God, who gives us the victory through our Lord Jesus Christ."

1

A Shattered Heart

"Sue, your mother is gone!" My husband, Marc, looked into my eyes with such compassion and sympathy as he repeated those very same words with a voice barely above a whisper. "Sue, your mother is gone!" His words stunned me to my very core as they began to permeate my understanding. Marc and I had worked for the same manufacturing company for many years in White Plains, Maryland. I was employed as a plant manager while Marc worked as a delivery driver. It was a typical, busy Monday morning at the plant. Parts of my daily responsibilities were overseeing the delivery process and ensuring Marc had his daily deliveries completed and loaded for the day ahead of him.

He left the plant anticipating a busy delivery schedule. After barely making it out to the main highway, Marc received an urgent call on his cell phone. We had just one cell phone at the time. I wanted him to carry it since he was out on the road. The call came from my youngest sister, Millie. She informed Marc my mother had suddenly passed away. Marc quickly turned the truck around and headed back to the plant with the tragic news.

When I initially saw that Marc had returned, I assumed I may have missed one of his deliveries, but that wouldn't be the case.

I stood there shocked and speechless. I desperately searched Marc's face, hoping to find the slightest hint that I had misunderstood what he had just told me; but when I saw the tears welling up in his eyes, it only confirmed that Mom had indeed died! Marc embraced me as the first agonizing wave of grief enveloped me. My legs threatened to buckle and give way. "She can't be gone," I cried. My heart shattered into a million pieces. It was May 9, 2005, the day after Mother's Day!

We had spent the previous weekend visiting Millie and her family in Pennsylvania. I had purchased a gift for the occasion while we were there. If anyone knew my mother, and I did, she enjoyed getting gifts. She would subtly drop hints before the gift-giving season approached. On our way back home from Pennsylvania that Sunday, I decided not to stop by my parents because of being tired from the trip. Instead, I would wait until the next day to give Mom her gift. Little did I know that gift exchange would never become a reality. I would never get to see her face light up with joy as she opened her gift.

I felt so selfish and guilt-ridden for not stopping the day before! Mom, I'm so sorry! Why didn't I stop!! Even more agonizing was the fact the opportunity was lost for one last "I love you, Mom" or one last hug! I suddenly thought of my father and how he had to be alone and grieving. I quickly turned to Marc and said, "We have to get to Dad! He's all alone, Marc!"

Getting to my dad became my central focus. Most of my siblings lived in Maryland, but they lived well over an hour away, so I knew with certainty he was alone. My anxiety and sorrow increased all the more as we left the plant and made the twenty-minute drive to my parents. The drive getting to my father seemed like an eternity. Memories of Mom started flooding my thoughts. Her smile, her laughter, and the sound of her voice had instantly become priceless. Treasures that would have to be remembered from this point on. I began to recall my last conversation with my mother four days prior. Even in my consuming grief, I became acutely aware of how God-ordained it was. The impact of her words suddenly hit me with astonishing revelation!

I will explain what I mean, but first allow me to suspend this moment while I share with you some of my family history involving this special woman I called my mother and how she played a crucial role in leading me to Jesus Christ, my Savior.

A Humble Beginning

My mother was commonly known as Jean throughout her life. It was a nickname she had acquired from her first name Regenia. She grew up very poor in the mountains of Millboro, Virginia. She met my father, Gerald Shryock (known as Jerry), who was from Cumberland, Maryland, through a mutual friend; and they soon started dating. After a relatively short courtship, my dad proposed, and they were married in a small church after moving to the quiet suburb of Beltsville, Maryland.

My mom was just fifteen years old, and my dad was twenty-three when they exchanged vows. They settled and made their starter home in Beltsville as well. My father became employed at a local lumber company as a carpenter building trusses for new construction homes. He was very good at working with wood, and he was also mechanically inclined. Although Dad was skillful at both, I would have to say his passion was working on cars, maybe borderline obsessive according to Mom. She would jokingly threaten my father that she was going to put a bed in his shed since that was where he spent much of his time. My mother soon discovered she was pregnant with her first child. After giving birth to Jerry, the rest of us followed in close succession. Next to be born was me (Sue), then Carol, Terry, Eugene, Alvin, and lastly, Millie. With seven children, my parents had their hands quite full. Dad's income was far from being sufficient to support a family of nine. My mother stayed at home and took care of her children.

Daily necessities such as food and clothing were hard to come by. Many times, our family relied on local charities and churches for food, shoes, and clothing. There were hard times in between when we went without meals. The house we lived in was a rental. The land-lord lived five houses up from us. When the landlord would show up to collect the monthly rent, Dad would send him away with a partial payment and a promise to pay the balance with the following week's paycheck. Dad always came up short financially. No matter where we lived, it was a common theme.

The humble little home we lived in had a total of four rooms: a living room, kitchen, and two bedrooms. It was extremely tight for a family the size of ours. Aside from inadequate space, it lacked many modern-day conveniences such as a furnace or any other type of heat-ing apparatus. Our heat source was an old wood-burning stove that was positioned two feet off the living room wall. It was also devoid of any indoor plumbing. Our water came from a well that was located in the backyard close to the house. The bathroom was outside, which was commonly called an outhouse.

Unlike the well that was conveniently located close to the house, the outhouse was situated at the very back of the yard near the edge of the woods! Go figure! Using the bathroom while being exposed to the harsh elements is never a pleasant experience for anyone, espe-cially a child. The darkness of night had its fair share of imaginary monsters lurking in the shadows! Let's not forget winter brrrrh!

Some of us kids learned to hold our water through the night, and some of the others, not so much! Having only two bedrooms to work with, my parents slept in one with my infant sister Millie while my five siblings and I slept in the other room. There was plenty of playing and fighting taking place at bedtime. With that many kids in one room, it inevitably came with the territory! That is until Dad would show up in the bedroom doorway with his all-too-familiar quote, "I DON'T WANT TO HEAR ONE MORE PEEP COMING FROM THIS ROOM!" which he always followed up with, "THE NEXT TIME, I'LL BE BRINGING MY BELT!" He may as well have been a cowboy from the wild west. My father could whip that belt off from around his waist like a professional gunslinger! Having previous experience, we knew he meant business. In light of that knowledge, we settled down and eventually fell asleep.

Even as a young child, it wasn't hard to see that my father stayed angry most of the time. It was out of that anger he disciplined his children, and it could be very painful! Dad didn't always use a belt, but when he did, we were left with bruised welts! Other times, we were thumped on the head with his knuckles, or he would grab a handful of hair and pull hard enough that you could hear the roots crack which always promised a lump. Sometimes Dad used his middle finger to poke us in the chest as a way to get his point across. That finger felt like steel, and it too left bruises! Staying out of my father's way was a high priority when it was unavoidable; I learned to walk on eggshells and did my best not to trigger his anger.

My mother and father argued often about his harsh discipline, but no fruitful changes ever seemed to come from their disagreements. Mom never harshly disciplined us, but it wasn't beyond her to grab a switch when she deemed it necessary. The very first time I ever heard the name Jesus was from my mother. She would often share the Bible stories with her children. I gleaned from my mom's teaching at a very young age that God was good, and Satan was evil.

One day, an older couple stopped by our home and knocked at our door. They greeted my mother with a warm friendly smile as she opened the door. "Hello! We are Mr. and Mrs. Stokes. We attend a small Baptist church less than a mile from here and would like to know if you would be interested in sending your children to Sunday school? We would be more than happy to pick them up and drop them off"!'

Mom was pleased with the offer and agreed to have me, Jerry, and Carol ready to go the next Sunday. Mom had the assurance that the gospel seeds she had planted in our hearts would be further watered while attending our new Sunday school. Being a former Christian preschool teacher, I can attest to the fact that children enjoy learning and are very receptive when taught the word of God. The Bible confirms this in PROVERBS 22:6, "TRAIN UP A CHILD IN

THE WAY HE SHOULD GO, AND WHEN HE IS OLD, HE WILL NOT DEPART FROM IT."

God's promise is the gospel seed is in the heart of a child permanently. Never to be forgotten! Their heart is fertile ground, making it good soil! As parents, it's our responsibility to plant good seeds. My mother planted the seed of God's promise in this child, and you will see the proof of that promise come to fruition in my life.

Up in Smoke

As Jerry, Carol, and I continued to attend Sunday school, the Bible began to come alive; and our knowledge about Jesus progressed. But there was another evil entity called the devil that my mother also told us about, and I knew with certainty I wanted nothing to do with him and his black heart. By the way, I still don't!

Early one summer morning at the age of four, I was outside playing in the healthy stuff called dirt. I had a twig and was using it to push and bully some black ants around. As I did, I happened to notice what I perceived to be suspicious-looking cracks in the ground. What wasn't obvious to an inquisitive four-year-old was the cracks were the result of a lack of rain, but I had my own little perspective on how they had gotten there. I ran as fast as my legs would take me into the house and straight to my mother! Out of breath and with excitement that was hard to contain, I said, "Mama!" When I was satisfied I had her full attention, I continued. "That devil tried to get up here last night while we were all sleeping."

First, you have to understand I believed the devil lived way down deep in the ground. I guess you could say he was under my feet! That part of my story was biblical. Mom, humoring me with wide-eyed wonder and mock surprise, replied, "He did?"

"Yep!" I confidently said, knowing I had the hard evidence outside a short distance away.

I proceeded to tell her about the cracks I had seen and that it proved what that sneaky devil tried to do the night before. After giving her my convincing account, I thought without a doubt she would follow me back outside to the crime scene; but to my bewilderment, she didn't budge from her chair though I did notice she restrained a giggle from behind her hand. I wouldn't comprehend her reaction to such a serious threat until many years later. Despite mom's lack of interest, I was determined to go back outside and keep a watchful eye on those cracks. God must have smiled as He nudged the Archangel Michael and said, "That's my little watchman in training." In HABAKKUK 2:1, "I WILL STAND ON MY GUARD POST AND STATION MYSELF ON THE RAMPART, AND I WILL SEE WHAT HE WILL SPEAK TO ME AND HOW I MAY RESPOND WHEN I AM REPROVED."

Although we were learning a great deal from Sunday school about God's commandments, the one about honoring your father and mother was coming at a much slower pace. In this case for Jerry, it was the obedient part of it he was going to break in a big way. My father forbade any of his children to touch the woodstove and for good reason. One winter morning after Dad left for work, Mom drove two miles down the road to my aunt's house in the hopes of getting some food for breakfast. After she left, the fire went out in our only heat source, the woodstove. With no insulation in a stick frame house, the temperature dropped rapidly. Since Mom wasn't there to start a fire, we would have to wait for her return and endure the teeth-chattering cold!

Jerry had another plan. He analyzed the situation and took it upon himself to start a fire in the stove. The plan may have been commendable and brave had Jerry been old enough to take on that type of responsibility, but at eight years old, he was hardly qualified to take on such a safety risk. I had to confess I wasn't willing to remind him he was breaking our father's strictest statute because I was freezing too! Besides, I reasoned, I wasn't the offender; Jerry was. Therefore, I had no guilt or fear.

Apparently, Jerry didn't either! After all, he had watched Dad start the fire in the stove many times; he had this down to a science! He continued on his mission to heat the house and added several pieces of wood to the stove. I chose to stand on the opposite side of the room instinctively knowing that the unfolding scenario had the potential to get very ugly! My thoughts were confirmed when I watched Jerry take down a small container of gasoline Dad kept on an upper shelf and pour—YES! I SAID POUR, copious amounts onto the wood. Carol stood to one side of the stove as she anticipated the soon coming heat.

Jerry struck the match and tossed it onto the gas-soaked wood. Instantly, there was a gigantic "POOF!" A large plume of black smoke immediately followed the explosion that left a big soot mark on the ceiling above the stove. When the smoke cleared, Carol and Jerry stood there with singed hair, eyelashes, and eyebrows to match! Their expressions begged the question, "What just happened?"

I, being the only eyewitness to the aftermath, took two positives away from the present situation. Number one, we had heat. Number two, I had nothing to do with it. Not even Mom was going to take this one lightly. A few moments later, Mom returned from my aunts and was shocked at what she was beholding. Next came the million-dollar question. "Who did it?" Jerry knew he was in deep trouble and that it would warrant breaking another commandment. He lied and blamed the explosion on Carol! Carol proclaimed her innocence, but Jerry was more convincing. Enter the dreaded switch, not the light on-off kind of switch but the bush kind! Poor Carol. It wasn't bad enough to have singed hair, eyelashes, and eyebrows; but getting a switching for something you're entirely innocent of is the worst! That's one switching to her credit she won't ever get to use for future disobedience.

To the best of my knowledge, I don't think Jerry ever attempted to start another fire in the stove, but I also believe he realized he narrowly escaped the penalty of Mom's switch, not to mention he could have burned the house down with all of us in it. A similar incident happened a few years prior with a distant neighbor who was a classmate of mine as well. Her older brother started a fire as she stood near the stove. Too much accelerant caused the fire to ignite the dress she was wearing. She survived, but the flames left her body terribly disfigured and scarred.

The winter months were painstakingly long for me and my brothers and sisters. We were rarely allowed to go outside to play due to Dad trying to keep the house warm. Every time a door was opened, it was an opportunity for a cold rush of winter air to come blasting in according to Dad. So that left us with Dad's heavy restrictions upon us in a four-room house. My father expected nothing less than quiet stillness when watching his favorite western shows. When things got too loud, and they did most of the time for Dad, he made us all sit shoulder to shoulder on the couch and then say his alltoo-familiar quote, "I don't want to hear one little peep coming from any of you!"

Not only was it unreasonable but also almost impossible! My brother Terry would pick that inopportune time to start the giggle game, and before long, we'd all be giggling uncontrollably despite Dad's warning. However, we were shown some mercy as Dad yelled a second warning. From that point on, we avoided all eye contact with Terry the instigator. There we were full of pent-up energy and nowhere to spend it. It was torture! Don't think about going to the bedroom and jumping on the bed for entertainment! Our only hope was an anticipation for an early spring.

The winter season also proved to be hard on my father. He experienced an accident on his job that left him incapacitated for several weeks. He had been with the lumber company for a few years now building roof trusses. After Dad completed a truss, the forklift driver transported the truss outside to the lumber yard where they were stacked until they reached a safe height. On one particular day, the forklift driver misjudged how high he had stacked the trusses, which resulted in the stack becoming unstable. Upon returning from a lunch break, Dad was walking through the lumber yard to get back to his workstation. As he walked past the stack of trusses, they started to sway. He was oblivious to the imminent danger he was facing. A coworker who was working nearby noticed the trusses were about to topple right on top of my father. The man had just enough time to yell two words in my dad's direction, "RUN, JERRY!" Sensing the danger, my father began running. He looked up momentarily and saw the huge stack of trusses that now threatened his very life! The trusses caught his right leg and broke his tibia bone in half. The break was brutal with part of the bone protruding from a hole in the skin, but dad was alive! If his coworker hadn't seen the impending danger and shouted a warning, my father would have been crushed to death!

After arriving home from school, Mom broke the news that Dad had an accident and was in the hospital. I was heartbroken! With tears streaming down my face, I asked her if he was going to be all right, and she assured me he would. In that moment, it didn't matter to me how hard or harsh my father was but how much I loved him. I loved him dearly and never desired to see him hurt in any way.

On the day he was released from the hospital, I was in school. When I got home and saw him sitting in his chair, I ran to him without hesitation and wrapped my arms around him with joyful tears running down my cheeks. Touched by my emotional display of love, my father gently smiled and returned my embrace. I cannot aptly put into words how loved I felt by my father in that treasured moment. It was like receiving an affirmation of his love that up to that point in my life Dad had never displayed to any of his children but, as a small child, I had constantly yearned for. It would be the only one I would get until adulthood.

Dad had a long recovery road ahead of him. His accident had taken place in the winter season, which made his trek back and forth to the bathroom (outhouse) on snow-covered icy ground treacherous on crutches with a cast up to his hip. He navigated his way with the constant threat of slipping and falling and possibly injuring himself further.

One bitter cold morning as Dad made the journey back from the bathroom and settled himself in his chair, Jerry came from the back door where he had watched Dad go out and come back in and said, "Daddy, someone knocked over our poop house!" Sorry, but those were his exact words. Dad had just laid his crutches on the floor beside his chair, and he looked at Jerry as if his imagination had gotten away from him and said, matter-of-factly, "Boy! I just came out of there. Now go sit down and be quiet." Dad wasn't in a mood to entertain Jerry or his wild imagination, but Jerry stood his ground and continued insisting that someone had knocked over our bathroom. Some of us went to the back door to have a look out the window and verify my brother's report, and sure enough, there was a car resting on the outhouse that now lay on its side. Dad grabbed his crutches to have a look for himself and was astonished to see it was exactly as Jerry had said. It was inconceivable to think that my father had just come from that small building moments before. What was more remarkable was in less than three weeks, Dad had come dangerously close to death two times!

I'm incredibly thankful God sees the danger ahead of time. Nothing in our life ever takes God by surprise because He has already been there. PSALM 139:16 says, "ALL THE DAYS ORDAINED FOR ME WERE WRITTEN IN YOUR BOOK BEFORE ONE OF THEM CAME TO BE." Meditate on this scripture for a moment. God has a book in heaven that He has personally authored about each one of us. You are a big deal to God! You may ask, "Does God truly love me that much?" The answer is a resounding yes! No one on this earth knows us more intimately than our creator.

LUKE 12:7 tells us He has every last hair on our head numbered and accounted for. You may also be wondering what God has written about you in His book. Ah! A destiny He planned for you before the foundation of the world was laid. When you make your decision to surrender your heart and give your life to "the author of life," He will begin to turn the pages of your book and reveal the destiny He has written about you. Here is a glimpse that is found in PSALM 139:17, "HOW PRECIOUS ARE YOUR THOUGHTS ABOUT ME GOD. THEY CANNOT BE NUMBERED." Like I said, you're a big deal to God.

God undoubtedly had His hand upon my father, and I am so thankful He did. Our neighbor called the police, and the driver was arrested and charged with driving while intoxicated. I wonder what the guilty offender has written in his book. After all, the accident could have ended much worse for him. Our outhouse, on the other hand, didn't fare so well! I guess you could say we were due for a bathroom remodel.

Your Story!

There is a book in heaven above
Authored by God in His merciful love

Each page was written with destiny and meaning
Before one day of your life came into being

They speak of His promises that are still to be told
His design for you that is yet to unfold

The title displays none other than your name
Specific to you no other can claim

Written with purpose by His majestic hand
From cover to cover its His perfect plan

Your life is precious and dear to Him
His promises for you await to begin

He beckons and calls, come read with me
Everything I've penned concerning your destiny

Surrender your will and you will discern
A beautiful journey with each page that He turns

In Psalm 139:16, "Your eyes saw my unformed body, all my days were written in your book and ordained for me before one of them came to be."

4

A Little Bit of Soap

The long-awaited spring season had arrived, and my siblings and I couldn't have been happier! We finally had the freedom to release a whole winter's worth of pent-up energy, and we hit the door running! Of course, the two golden rules still applied. "No running in and out" and "Don't let the screen door slam!" Those rules were enforced by my parents with the threat of making us stay inside. That was the last thing my brothers and sisters and I wanted to do.

One of the things at the top of our list was exploring. This often led us into the woods behind our house. In our explorations, we never stumbled onto any snakes, which was a plus! Mom was an avid bird lover. She especially enjoyed the songbirds. One of her treasured favorites was the cardinal. She often exclaimed about their beautiful red color although it was the males who were the brightly colored ones. I was inclined to agree with her. Knowing her love for birds, Dad would build birdhouses and place them in the trees around the yard along with a birdbath. Mom could easily watch from a window whenever her feathered friends came to take a turn splashing themselves or take residence in one of their new homes.

It amazed me how something so simplistic brought my mother such joy! During some of our explorations, we were guaranteed to come across a bird's nest with freshly hatched eggs. Mom gave me and my siblings strict orders to never touch or get close enough to breathe on the nest. She feared the mother bird would abandon her young if she could detect a human scent. Mom was adamant about this, and she backed it up with a switch warning, making the eggs kid-proof.

As the days grew warmer with the approaching summer season, the bees and wasps were becoming very active. Jerry discovered this in a very painful way. He was playing in the woods and accidentally stumbled on a nest of unforgiving yellow jackets! He came out of the woods screaming at breakneck speed with the aggressive wasps swarming him. He was being stung multiple times! My mother and a neighbor managed to get the wasps off by stripping him out of his clothes since that was where most of the wasps had attached themselves. I felt sorry for Jerry, but at the risk of sounding selfish again, I was glad it wasn't me!

The warmer weather kept my father in his favorite habitat, his shed! The coldness of winter proved to be hard on the mended bone in his leg. It also left him with a permanent limp, but he never let it slow him down. He spent hours catching up on many anticipated projects whether it was wood or the mechanical side of it. Just like the stove, Dad's children were forbidden to touch anything in his shed. The only time we were allowed in his shed is if he sent one of us to fetch a tool for him. A shed was a must-have for my father even if he had to build it himself, which he did on several occasions. The only exception was when it came to apartment living.

Another early childhood memory I recall of Mom was that she played guitar. She never had a single guitar lesson, but she managed to teach herself how to play, and that was an amazing accomplishment for me. As she put it, "I learned to play by ear." I would watch as she strummed her guitar and sang the old hymns with tears streaming down her face. I instinctively knew even from a young age that these tears were different. They didn't come from sorrow or sadness, but they were tears of worship, love, and adoration for her Lord.

Our home kept a constant atmosphere of stress, tension, and anxiety due to Dad's anger. When Mom played and sang the hymns, it always had a calming effect on my father as he lingered nearby to listen. It was one of the rare moments I could notice the positive influence it had on him. A sense of peace would come over my father.

After getting older, I came to understand that my mother's worship changed the atmosphere in our home to one that invited the Holy Spirit's presence. The Bible tells us in PSALM 22:3, "GOD INHABITS THE PRAISES OF HIS PEOPLE." His peace was always a welcome change in our little home whenever Mom sang and worshiped. Those moments were treasurable but short-lived. As I expressed before, my father was angry most of the time. As one of his children, I found it difficult to distinguish between right and wrong where it concerned my dad since almost everything we did was wrong! It wasn't any different for my siblings. We were never given a chance to ask the question, "What exactly was my offense?" Clear boundaries were never established, and that made our borders open for interpretation. Most of the time, we got it wrong!

Dad's anger was accompanied by an extensive vocabulary that included a lot of cuss words he used quite frequently. I was a curious child who never missed much that was going on around me. I began taking mental notes of all those cuss words Dad would angrily spew out, and I stored them away in my little memory bank. I was on the playground one day with my first-grade class when I started using those offensive words. Every time a classmate cut me off at the slide or swing, there I was, using profanity! I was completely clueless, at that age, about the meaning of these offensive words. I just knew they were used when you got angry like my father. It didn't take long for my offended classmates to tell the teacher. My teacher requested a conference with my mother. We didn't have a phone, so my teacher sent a letter home to Mom by "yours truly!" After reading the request, Mom asked me, "Why does your teacher want a conference with me? What did you do?"

I shrugged while replying, "I don't know." The truth was, I really didn't, or I would have thought twice about giving her the letter.

After the conference with my teacher, it was clear Mom wasn't happy about it, and neither was I. When Dad was told about the situation, he was only too eager to dole out the discipline. He sat me on a stool in the kitchen and retrieved a bar of Ivory soap. Oh, no! I knew what was coming and wasn't good! "Open your mouth!" I reluctantly opened my mouth, and he told me to bite down on the soap. I can't express how nasty it was! I cried and gagged, then gagged some more to the point of vomiting! I almost would have rather had the woodshed, ALMOST! After a few tortuous minutes, my father asked me, "Are you going to cuss anymore?"

I assured him I was done with cussing by shaking my head no! Then he removed the soap. I couldn't get to the trash can quick enough to spit out the residual nastiness!

PROVERBS 22:15 says, "A CHILD'S HEART HAS THE TENDENCY TO DO WRONG, BUT THE ROD OF DISCIPLINE REMOVES IT FAR FROM HIM." Not the soap, Dad! It only traumatized me every time I saw a bar of Ivory after that. I can still taste it! Besides, I never witnessed my father eating any of it. I wasn't about to bring that point up to Dad. There was still plenty of Ivory left.

5

Moving Up

One of my third-grade classmates named Bonnie lived two doors down from me. She and I occasionally played together. Bonnie's family lived in a very nice well-to-do home with a large pool in the backyard. As a young child, I was often envious when I saw how fortunate Bonnie and her family were. They had things I could only dream about as a child. One day, Bonnie and I were playing at the edge of her backyard near the woods when her mother called Bonnie's name from the back door. Bonnie responded by letting her mom know she was in the back near the woods. What happened next would emotionally scar me for years to come!

Her mother yelled back and asked, "What are you doing back there?"

Bonnie replied, "I'm playing with Sue."

In a very reprimanding tone, her mother said, "What did I tell you about playing with that trash? Get in this house right now!"

I was devastated at her cutting words! Bonnie and I were both speechless for a moment, and then I looked at her and said, "Why did your mom call me trash?"

She was visibly uncomfortable and embarrassed by her mother's cruel statement. Bonnie responded in the only way she knew how, "I don't know. I have to go in now."

As I slowly made my way home, I kept hearing those painful words over and over in my head. She thought of me as nothing more than a refuse! I felt hurt and was on the brink of crying.

There is an adage that used to be very popular with children: "Sticks and stones can break my bones but names will never hurt me!" Quite the opposite is true! They can break your heart! Numerous studies and articles, written by mental health experts, have proven name-calling has many adverse effects on children. Some of those are having low self-esteem and low confidence levels. Their self-worth is greatly diminished and can encourage violent outbursts to name a few.

When I got home I informed my mother about the incident. She was furious enough to bite nails in half! She angrily stomped her way down to Bonnie's house being fully cocked and loaded to give Bonnie's mother a piece of her mind. Judging by Mom's demeanor, the issue wasn't going to be resolved in a civilized or sanctified manner! There was a fence that separated Bonnie's yard from the neighbor, which was a positive in this situation since it served as a barrier between Mom and Bonnie's mother. Mom would have stood toe-to-toe with her if that fence hadn't been there.

After a brief altercation and a stiff warning from my mother not to ever call her child trash again, Mom spat out the nails and headed back home. I believe Ivory soap may have been in order after that confrontation, but just like dad, I wasn't going there with Mom! I had to admit I felt vindicated. As I followed Mom back home, I resisted the urge to turn around and stick my tongue out at Bonnie's mother. From that point on, I stayed in my yard and never ventured near Bonnie's yard again per my mother!

We remained friends and talked with each other at school, but that was the extent of our friendship. The day after the confrontation, I overheard my mother telling the neighbor next door that being poor didn't make our family trash. As a child, I was unable to comprehend why being poor made a person trash. It did not compute in my childlike mind. What it did do is plant a hurtful seed in my heart that followed me into my adulthood, and it eventually produced a root of bitterness.

HEBREWS 12:15 tells us, "SEE TO IT NO ONE COMES SHORT OF THE GRACE OF GOD, THAT NO ROOT OF BITTERNESS SPRINGING UP, CAUSES TROUBLE, AND BY IT MANY BE DEFILED." God dealt with me about that bitter root of unforgiveness forty years later. I was watching a pastor on television speaking on the bitter root of unforgiveness. He said, "A person may be harboring this root without realizing it, so ask the Lord to search your heart." After doing a quick inventory of my heart, I was convinced that I wasn't harboring any bitter roots. Then I asked the Lord, "Lord, do I have any unforgiveness in my heart?"

I was shocked when He brought Bonnie's mother to my attention! "Really, Lord?"

Then He said, "How many times over the years have you thought about looking her up and confronting her about what she called you as a child?"

I had to admit; it was more times than I had fingers and toes! There was just one thing left to do; I made the heart decision to forgive her, and I did that day. We can't trust ourselves to search our hearts! No one and nothing knows our heart like the divine creator! In PSALM 139:23, "SEARCH ME GOD, AND KNOW MY HEART, TRY ME, AND KNOW MY THOUGHTS."

The landlord informed my parents that he had sold the property and that we had to move. Finding a home for a family of nine would be a difficult task. Dad struggled to pay the rent for our four-room home! My parents did manage to locate another rental property in Beltsville, and it was considerably larger. The new property had two stories and three bedrooms. The real excitement for our family in the new house was it had indoor plumbing! It may seem strange to some that we would get so excited over indoor plumbing, but if you have never had to go outside to use the bathroom or to get daily water from a well, then you can't share in the excitement!

A larger home meant higher monthly rent. Dad decided to take in a boarder to help with the rent. Mom never worked, which put the entire financial burden on my father's shoulders. For reasons I never came to realize, my mother lacked the confidence to work outside the home, which was unfortunate for my father. The enormity of the financial burden alone had to be part of the reason Dad stayed angry most of the time! It had to be like living in a vise that only got continually tighter and more stressful for him.

Our new backyard was massive! At the back edge of the yard was a creek that was begging to be explored, and explore we did. The creek was only about a foot deep, but we discovered it was a habitat for crayfish and minnows. My siblings and I enjoyed catching them in jars and then releasing them back into the water. Another huge perk was a corner store located directly across the street. Back in the seventies, small corner stores sold penny candy and eight-cent fudgesicles! It doesn't get any better than that for a kid! I know I'm giving away my age here. I also discovered you could get a two-cent return deposit on an empty soda bottle, so I would search for discarded bottles on the side of the road throughout our neighborhood and return them to the store for the deposit, which I eagerly spent on a penny candy.

Although we still resided in Beltsville, we had moved out of our old school district. My siblings and I would be starting new schools in the fall, and that was something I wasn't looking forward to! Meeting new classmates and making new friends had my anxiety alarm going off! Despite my apprehension, when the time came to start school, I acclimated to my new school quite well and was making new friends. One of those friends was Cheryl who happens to be in my class. She lived just two streets over from me. I would go over to her house to hang out from time to time. Cheryl had an older stepsister named Debbie who eventually became my best friend. Debbie was three years older than me, but despite the age gap, our friendship was almost instantaneous. She had stacks of forty-five records that we would sit and listen to. Debbie always had the latest record hits on vinyl.

Mom found a church close by that we started attending. In my mother's words, it was a "Holy Ghost-filled church!" She wouldn't have it any other way. My father wanted no part of what he considered to be a Holy Roller church, and he let my mom know that in an Ivory soap kind of way, but she didn't let Dad's resistance stop her from praying for him. She often requested prayer for his salvation in the church services. His rantings seemed to be getting worse.

One night after coming home from church, Dad went into a full-throttle rant, and it was targeted at Mom. He was yelling and cursing when all of a sudden Mom stood up with righteous indignation and said "Satan! I rebuke you in the name of Jesus!" Dad stood there in stunned silence for a moment, then retreated upstairs to the bedroom without another swear word! My mother recognized all too well who was at work through my father. Using her God-given authority, she stood her ground and said, "No more!"

JAMES 4:7 tells us, "SUBMIT YOURSELVES THEREFORE TO GOD, RESIST THE DEVIL, AND HE WILL FLEE FROM YOU." It wouldn't be the last time Satan would use my father for his attacks against Mom. Having a front-row seat, I can testify that the attacks were verbally brutal, and I could see where they began to take a toll on my mother. Her church attendance began to gradually taper off until she and her children eventually stopped going altogether.

6

Hard Times Continue

Although we now lived in a more modern up-to-date home, many things remained unchanged, one of those things being the financial strain that affected us all! It seemed to get progressively worse if that were possible. The boarder moved out, and Dad was, again, scraping to meet the monthly rent. Just as in times past, he consistently sent the landlord away with an explanation of hardship and a promise to pay with his next paycheck. I held a level of compassion for my father because of his constant struggle to keep his family afloat. He worked hard but never attained his goal of having enough to pay the bills. He still worked for the lumber company, but his raises were minimal.

The first winter in our new home proved to be every bit as cold as the previous home. We had an oil furnace in the basement, but the funds for the oil weren't always there. When the oil was purchased, it came at the expense of another bill. Without oil, the house became cold enough to see the fog of your breath from inside! We layered as many blankets as we could, but it was still miserably cold! Again we were left with the hope of an early spring. Getting ready for school in a frigid environment was harsh! The hot-water heater was broken, but Dad dared not approach the landlord about it for fear of him demanding the back rent. So we heated bathwater in pots on the kitchen stove. We didn't own a washer or dryer. We hand-washed our school clothes the night before and hoped they would be dry by morning, and that was providing we had heat!

The money for our much-needed school supplies was nonexistent. My teacher would ask me in front of the whole class why I never came to school prepared. Not wanting to be embarrassed or mocked by the other kids, I shrugged my shoulders with indifference and refused to answer. It was better than admitting my parents didn't have the money. I knew all too well how cruel kids could be!

Carol and I took turns doing dish duty. There was always a mountain of dirty dishes because we both avoided them like the plague. Dish detergent wasn't readily available, but bars of Ivory soap were! My father and Ivory had an unbreakable bond. We would rub the bar of soap onto a dishcloth and wash the dishes as best as we could. It would take Carol and me forever and a day to do those dishes! Dad arrived home from work one day in a very disgruntled mood. Carol had not washed the dishes yet which sent Dad into a rage! He took the steps leading upstairs to our room, two at a time, and flung the bedroom door open. He grabbed a handful of Carol's hair and pulled her by her hair down the stairs as she screamed and cried, "Daddy, stop! You're hurting me," but to no avail.

He angrily jerked her head back and forth the whole way down the stairs until he got her in front of the sink and said, "Now get these dishes done!" Dad's vicious attack left Carol with a baseball-sized bald spot on the back of her head. She was traumatized! Mom wasn't home at the time, but I knew with certainty if she had been there, the tragic situation wouldn't have taken place! When she returned home and saw the abuse Dad had done to Carol, Mom became very confrontational with my father, and they almost came to physical blows! Carol kept that clump of hair in a container for years as a reminder of what my father had done to her.

Carol and I would earn extra money by raking the yard of an elderly woman who lived up the street from us. She had a huge yard that took us all day to complete. Our final pay was seventy-five cents apiece. Sometimes the money we earned bought minimal school supplies or paid for a school trip, but most of the time, we spent our hard-earned money at the corner store. Food remained a rare commodity in our home. We often went to school without any breakfast, but we did get a hot lunch at school since we were enrolled in the free lunch program. Getting a hot dinner at home was few and far between. Most of the time, dinner consisted of a bologna sandwich. Don't get me wrong, it was better than going hungry, and it took the guesswork out of what we were having for dinner.

The power company shut our electricity off numerous times for nonpayment. Sometimes the power would be off for months at a time. At the risk of repeating myself, you can't appreciate things in life until you have to do without them. My father had these old oil lamps that we used for lighting. The winter months with no heat were long enough, but minus the electricity made it unbearable. Then one morning, you venture outside, and there it was! Glorious spring with the warmth of the sun hitting your face! Every bird in the neighborhood was singing in a joyful celebration! In SOLOMON 2:11, "FOR BEHOLD, THE WINTER IS PAST, THE RAIN IS OVER AND GONE."

Dad made it out to his beloved shed, doing what he loved best, his projects! He put a bicycle together for each one of us from discarded frames that others had thrown out as trash. He always saw the potential of turning one man's trash into another man's treasure. Having a bike of our own was like Christmas to me and my siblings. It never bothered us that our bikes came from used parts. As long as they got us from point A to point B, we were thrilled. The only negative for me was coming outside with the anticipation of a long bike ride, only to discover Jerry had taken my ride because his bike had a flat! Ugh! That meant whatever plans I had for the day, I would be doing them walking!

It had been a while since Mom had attended church, but I would often hear her listening to a radio preacher by the name of R. W. Schambach. She loved his fiery style of preaching. His boldness in preaching the gospel was captivating to me, so I would sometimes sit and listen with Mom. After the radio program, I became curious about the sermon and ask her questions about the Bible. I could tell it pleased her, and she was only too eager to answer my questions.

I would witness her praying and reading God's word many times. I knew Mom had a deep abiding love for the Lord, but I secretly wished she would go back to church. Mom was given a parakeet by a friend, and she was ecstatic with her new feathered friend.

She named him Petey and wasted no time in training him to talk and whistle. She was attached at the heart level. It was just Mom and Petey when all of us kids were at school. She remarked about how Petey kept her good company throughout the day.

These little birds were very fragile when it came to their health. During the winter months when we had no heat, Mom made sure Petey's cage was covered so he wouldn't get sick. This protective cover worked for several years until one winter the cold temperature took its toll on Petey. He got very sick and died! My mother was crushed over losing her friend. She mourned and cried over that little bird for weeks! The whole family was deeply saddened. Petey had been a part of our home for seven years.

In time, we acquired another pet in the form of a dog. He was a Shepherd who was given to Jerry by one of his friends. He already had the given name of Poncho, so that's what we continued to call him. He was a nicelooking dog, and we all wondered why his original owner gave him away. After a short time, Poncho started to exhibit some strange behavior that indicated he may not be a very intelligent canine. To give this statement some credence, my brothers and sisters and I witnessed a strange habit he had. Poncho liked to eat rocks! As bizarre as that sounds, it was true! It was even weirder to watch him do it! He obviously wasn't able to chew the stone, but if you tossed him a medium-sized rock, he would catch it mid-air in his mouth and swallow it whole. He was great entertainment for our friends whenever they came over. At first, they wouldn't believe it until we had Poncho demonstrate his skill or lack thereof. Every time my father mowed the grass, he could always tell where Poncho left his deposits. You could hear multiple stones hitting the mower blades with Dad shaking his fist and cursing the dog.

Poncho wandered through the neighborhood at will, which means he wouldn't allow anyone to tether him. One growl from him, and it was, "Okay, have it your way!" Trying to keep him out of traffic was a task. Another example of his low-doggie IQ was that he took some of his naps in the middle of the street in front of our house! Whenever we heard car horns blaring and people shouting, we knew it had to be Poncho sleeping on the double yellows! He may have started the whole road-rage movement. Had to be the rocks, I guess! Despite his lack of intelligence, he was firmly established as part of our family.

My mother finally decided to go back to church. One Sunday after church, we discovered Poncho lying on the front steps of the church. Our pastor joked and said we now have a Holy Ghost-filled dog. I believe God was looking out for that crazy rock-eating dog because although the church was a quarter mile from home, the street Poncho crossed to get to the church was heavily traveled. Interestingly enough, Poncho would prove to be a testimony to our church and to others confirming that God truly did have His protective hand on our dog.

7

Our Miracle Dog!

My grandparents on my father's side lived in Cumberland, Maryland. It was a three-and-half-hour trip one way by car. Dad decided to take a family trip one summer weekend to visit the grandparents. We were all very excited since road trips were a rare treat! As a child, I was always fascinated to see the majestic beauty of the mountains in western Maryland. We were all super excited to visit the grandparents. All nine of us loaded into the car and were more than ready to get our trip started. Dad put the car in reverse and started backing out of the driveway when suddenly, we heard a strange dragging sound. It seemed to be coming from beneath the car. Dad assumed it had to be a twig that had fallen from a nearby tree and that it would gradually loosen and break free.

He put the car in reverse again and began backing up, but the noise didn't subside as he had presumed. Perplexed, Dad put the vehicle in park and got out to have a thorough look underneath. He immediately discovered the source of the noise and started yelling frantically, "GET OUT OF THE CAR! IT'S PONCHO!" Poncho had been lying beneath the car to escape the summer heat. When our entire family loaded in the car, the total weight brought the car down to a level that wouldn't allow him to squeeze out from underneath! Poncho was trapped! As my father was backing up, it caused Poncho's hind legs to curl unnaturally over his head much like a ball, and that ball position was what he was presently trapped in! Dad retrieved the car jack from the trunk and desperately started jacking the car up! Everyone was now standing outside the car, crying and hoping our dog was still alive, and then we heard his painful whimpers.

By this time, we were all on our hands and knees trying to coax Poncho out, but we could see that his front paw had somehow gotten lodged in the bottom of the car. He was trying to free himself while yelping in pain at the same time. At last, he pulled his paw free and began to scoot himself out from underneath. He was frightened and in shock. He tried to run and fell repeatedly as he yelped in pain. Our hearts were breaking for him! It was visibly clear he had some serious injuries. His front legs were functioning, but not his hind legs. Poncho collapsed in a heap, helpless to do anything but tremble and whimper. He looked so pitiful! How ironic to think of the many times he napped in the street or crossed a dangerous road to get to the church, only to be injured in the safety of his own driveway.

Dad wrapped Poncho in some blankets then gently picked him up and laid him on the back seat of the car and took him to the local veterinarian's hospital. After a complete examination and some x-rays, the veterinarian confirmed Poncho's back was severely broken. So bad, in fact, he would never walk again. He advised my dad that it would be best to put him down. My father wasn't prepared to make that decision without first talking to Mom. He left Poncho there while he came back home to give my mother the grim news. She wouldn't hear of it and sent my father back to the animal hospital to get our dog.

The vet thought my parents were crazy, but he did give Dad some pain medicine for Poncho. My mother was about to take a giant leap of faith. At the Thursday night church service that same week, Mom had a very special prayer request. The dog that rested on the front church steps needed a miracle, and she needed the rest of the church to believe with her, and they did! The Lord cares about all of His creation, and He expects us to do the same. PROVERBS 12:10 says, "A RIGHTEOUS MAN CARES FOR THE NEEDS OF HIS ANIMALS."

Our pastor and the church members didn't hesitate to pray and believe for a miracle for our dog. In a few short weeks, Poncho was completely healed and was walking again just as well as he did before his injury! God honored my mother's faith, and He delivered big! Mom testified before the congregation about Poncho's miracle, and there was rejoicing and celebration!

There was one person left who needed to see and hear about our dog's miraculous healing, and my father would be the one doing the witnessing! With Poncho in tow, Dad drove back to the veterinarian's hospital. When the vet came out to the front reception desk, my father looked at him and asked, "Do you remember this dog?" as he pointed at Poncho.

The vet looked puzzled and replied, "I'm sorry, but no I don't!"

Dad explained, "This is the dog I brought to you a few weeks ago with a broken back that you said would never walk again!"

Then the vet said, "Oh, yes! I do recall that dog."

My father said, "This is the same dog!"

The doctor looked at Poncho incredulously as he stood on all four legs. "There is no way that could be the same dog," the doctor replied!

Dad confidently stated, "He most certainly is, and I want you to know that through prayer and faith, the Lord healed this dog!" Dad left with the vet scratching his head, but more importantly with the irrefutable proof of the healing power of Jesus standing before him on all four legs. As you can tell, Poncho's recovery had an impact on my father as well. He wasn't willing just yet to surrender his life to the Lord, but the callousness of his heart was surely touched.

If God is more than willing to heal our pets, how much more willing is He to heal us of every sickness, disease, and emotional trauma? The Bible tells us in MATTHEW 8:1–3,

LARGE CROWDS FOLLOWED JESUS AS HE CAME DOWN THE MOUNTAINSIDE. SUDDENLY, A MAN WITH LEPROSY APPROACHED HIM AND KNELT BEFORE HIM. "LORD, THE MAN SAID, IF YOU ARE WILLING, YOU CAN HEAL ME AND MAKE ME CLEAN." JESUS REACHED OUT AND TOUCHED HIM. "I AM WILLING" HE SAID. "BE HEALED"! AND INSTANTLY THE LEPROSY DISAPPEARED.

God is always willing if we are willing to believe and stand on His promises. MARK 9:23 confirms this. "JESUS SAID TO HIM, IF YOU CAN BELIEVE, ALL THINGS ARE POSSIBLE TO HIM WHO BELIEVES." There have been moments of reflection in my life where I could clearly see that God's hand of protection was upon me. One such moment came when I was twelve years old. Mom had cooked a fried chicken dinner, one of my favorite meals! It was summer, and my brothers and sisters and I hurried outside after dinner to play hide-and-seek. We had been playing for a while when I called for a time out to go inside and get some water. On my way back outside, I glanced over at the table and noticed a leftover chicken breast on a plate. Eagerly wanting to get back to the game, I quickly grabbed the breast and tore off a piece and shoved it in my mouth. Because I was in a rush, I didn't adequately chew the meat before swallowing, and the chicken lodged securely in my throat completely blocking my airway.

I immediately panicked! There wasn't anyone in the house that could render any type of aid! Dad was in his shed, and my mother had left to go to my grandmother's house down the street. I was alone and in deep trouble! Thoughts came rushing to my mind, *This is how you're going to die! You're going to choke to death on a piece of chicken!*

It was at that very moment I heard a calm voice from somewhere deep inside of me speak one word, "COUGH!" I couldn't get any air in, but I could force out a cough; and when I did, that piece of chicken came flying out onto the floor! I took in a much-needed breath of glorious air! After getting my composure and breathing back to normal, all I could think about was how close I just came to death and how I wouldn't make that mistake again no matter how appetizing that chicken looked.

Many years later, I thought about the voice I had heard that saved my life that day. I have come to know Him as the Holy Spirit. The book of JOHN tells us in verse 10:27, "MY SHEEP HEAR MY VOICE." I am so thankful to be one of His sheep!

When I finally returned outside to the game, I tried telling my siblings about my neardeath experience, but all they said was, "You're it, and we're hiding!"

8

From Rebellion to Brokenness, Back to Rebellion

By the time I reached my teens, my friends and music had become a high priority in my life. I discovered that being a *Jesus freak*, as you were labeled in the seventies culture, wasn't very popular with my friends. I started to conveniently disappear when it was time to attend church. It didn't take Mom long to notice my indifferent (rebellious) attitude when it came to going to church, and she voiced those concerns to me.

I stiffened my neck and argued there were other things I'd rather do instead. Mom wasn't about to give up, and I wasn't budging an inch! On the surface, this headstrong confrontation appeared to be a battle of our will, but Mom had a much greater weapon that I knew nothing about, and it would work to her advantage. It was called prayer! Like many God-fearing mothers, she was praying for me. James 5:16 says, "The earnest prayer of a righteous person has great power and produces wonderful results." In other words, I didn't stand a chance!

At fourteen, I was ignorant of just how powerful her prayers were, but I was about to find out. On one particular day, Mom casually mentioned to me, "The church is having a revival this week, and I really would like for you to go with me." I instantly recoiled at the mere suggestion of going. It had been a while since she had asked me to attend church, so I figured she had given up, and I had won the battle. That wouldn't be the case!

"I already have plans to meet up with friends later on," I replied. My important plans consisted of going two streets over to hang out with Debbie. I didn't want to go to church, much less a revival.

Mom was defiantly holding her ground, and her casual attitude went out the window. "You can either go to the revival with me tonight, or you can stay home without going anywhere!"

"What! That's hardly fair!" I protested as I stomped my feet!

"That's it! Take it or leave it," she countered.

Those were my options, and I thought, *They stunk!* I knew for sure I didn't want to stay home; hence, I was grudgingly going to a revival. But I would be going with a stiff-necked, rebellious attitude, and I would make certain my mother felt the chilly atmosphere for making me go! Then, I suddenly had an idea! "Hey, Mom, can I go to Debbie's to see if she would like to go with us?"

Mom was pleased with the idea and granted my request. So off I went to Debbie's house with the hope she would want to go. *If I had to go, it would be more tolerable having my best friend with me*, I thought. Although I was hopeful, I honestly didn't think she would take me up on my offer given the fact she was just as rebellious as I was. Yep! She was quite the hero to me! To my utter amazement, Debbie accepted my invitation! Small miracle? Perhaps, but the biggest unexpected miracles were yet to unfold that night!

My sister Carol decided she would go too. When the time came to leave for the service, Mom did something strange. She got in on the passenger side of the car instead of the driver's seat. As I was getting ready to question her motives, my father walked out of the house in dressed clothes. I was shocked! I turned to Mom and said, "No way! Dad is going?"

My mother smiled in affirmation. I was completely dumbfounded! My father was going to church, amazing! Upon reconsideration, I wouldn't miss going to this revival for the world, pardon the pun! It just keeps getting better and better. The rebellion I was feeling earlier had turned to excitement! It was the first time in my life I had ever witnessed my father going to church, and that for me was a huge deal! Dad slid into the driver's seat, and we were on our way. I was seeing the fruit of my mother's fervent prayers being answered, and the night wasn't over yet.

When we arrived at the church, the parking lot was already becoming packed in anticipation of the revival, but Dad managed to find a space to park. As we entered the sanctuary, the atmosphere felt charged with excitement and expectation. There were many new faces seated in the pews that had come to hear the visiting evangelist. I also saw the surprise and delight of the church members as my father walked in with my mother. They were very familiar with my mom's many prayer requests concerning Dad's salvation.

We found a seat in one of the pews, and within minutes, the praise and worship started. Being the teenagers that we were, Debbie, Carol, and I chose a seat behind the parents. It wasn't long before Mom was consumed in the Spirit. I knew from previous experience that Mom was an exuberant worshiper, which meant she would spontaneously throw her hands in the air at any given "hallelujah" moment.

Dad was clueless about how Mom worshiped and then, it happened! Mom threw her hands up in the air accompanied by a "hallelujah" and hit my father in the face with the back of her hand. Debbie, Carol, and I giggled from the pew behind careful that Dad didn't see or hear us, but it was hilarious! He gave Mom a stern look that she was oblivious to. Wanting to safeguard himself for the next hallelujah, Dad put a distance of three feet between himself and my mother.

The visiting evangelist began his fiery sermon, and soon a conviction went out over the audience. Some people were on their feet in jubilant praise while others sat with tears running down their cheeks. Still, others were eyeing the back door as a way of escape, myself included! At the end of the sermon, an altar call for repentance went out over the audience. It was so quiet in that church you could hear a pin drop. The atmosphere was heavy with the convicting power of the Holy Spirit, almost tangible!

One by one people began making their way to the altar. I would be lying if I said my heart wasn't being stirred and convicted, but

I planned to stay planted right where I was with my head lowered and my eyes focused on the floor in front of me. I dared not make eye contact with anyone, especially the pastor making the altar call! I desperately wanted to escape by slipping out the back door of the church.

The pastor continued with the repentance call as people continued coming forward. *Why can't he finish the call already!* I thought. *I should have stayed home!* The convicting power of the Holy Spirit only intensified, and I was struggling to conceal the effect it was having on me! This was not supposed to be happening! What if Debbie sees me like this? My rebellious reputation would be over! I falsely assured myself that the service would be ending soon and to just hang in there, but the tears welling up in my eyes were betraying me as they ran down my cheeks. I quickly wiped them away and tried swallowing the huge lump in my throat.

It was then that I saw movement in front of me as I looked up from the floor. Dad stood with tears streaming down his face. *What was he doing?* I thought. He started to make his way down to the altar! My father was broken and undone. I couldn't believe what I was seeing! A man I've known all my life to be angry, who cursed his wife, who physically abused his children for the least provocation, was now standing before the altar overwhelmed by the love of the Holy Spirit, ready to give his heart to Jesus!

Never underestimate the loving power of God to soften even the hardest of hearts. Witnessing this magnificent display of love the Spirit had on my father was truly miraculous. I was overcome and touched to my very core! What little fight I had left in me was swallowed up by the love of the Holy Spirit. He wholly consumed and enveloped my heart. I waved my white flag in total beautiful surrender. At the age of fourteen, this rebellious teenager, like her father, was broken and undone.

If you have to lose a battle, let it be this one! Psalm 51:17 tells us, "My sacrifice to God is a broken spirit, a broken and contrite heart, such, O God, you will not despise." I slowly stood to my feet just as my father had done moments earlier and walked down to the altar with tears flowing unabated. I was no longer concerned about my composure or my rebellious reputation. One of the altar servants quickly came over to me and led me through the sinner's prayer.

After I received Jesus as my Lord and Savior, something very unexpected happened. I started speaking in a language I had never known before! I had no idea what I was speaking, but I did know it was a glorious experience! I was filled with joy! I overheard someone say with excitement, "She's being baptized in the Holy Spirit!"

All I knew with certainty was that my conversation was between me and the Almighty! 1 CORINTHIANS 14:2 says, "FOR ONE WHO SPEAKS IN A TONGUE DOES NOT SPEAK TO MEN BUT TO GOD." I know there may be some who do not believe in this prayer language, but for me, my experience has left no doubt that it was genuine. I wasn't seeking God for it, but He, and He alone, saw fit to empower me with this experience.

The entire church was in a jubilant uproar! Many people had given their lives to the Lord that night. The atmosphere was one of joyful celebration for the miracles of salvation! As I glanced to my right for the first time after coming forward, it was then I realized my sister Carol and my best friend Debbie were standing before the altar and had given their lives to the Lord as well! I was worried about keeping my conviction concealed and didn't realize the Lord was also convicting their hearts in the same moment.

Each of us including my father had a divine appointment that night. I spotted my mom, and she was having a "thankful-hallelujah" party all by herself. Her husband, two daughters, and her daughter's best friend had given their lives to the heavenly kingdom. Heaven was in a jubilant celebration too! In LUKE 15:10, "IN THE SAME WAY, I TELL YOU, THERE IS REJOICING IN THE PRESENCE OF THE ANGELS OF GOD OVER ONE SINNER WHO REPENTS." Just one person coming to Christ makes for a joyous celebration party in heaven! That's how much God loves us! We are all a big deal to Him! He tells us in REVELATION 3:20, "BEHOLD, I STAND AT THE DOOR AND KNOCK. IF ANYONE HEARS MY VOICE AND OPENS THE DOOR I WILL COME IN AND EAT WITH HIM AND HE WITH ME." Love came knocking, and four hearts answered the door.

After that revival night, I continued to attend church and other revivals with Mom for a while. I would love to say my spiritual journey continued to progress, but unfortunately, it didn't. I caved to the peer pressure and wasn't fond of being called a *Jesus freak*. Carol stayed with her journey longer than I did, but in time, she too caved to peer pressure. Dad had slipped back into his old ways as well. Debbie, the real rebellious one, continued in her newfound journey and became a youth pastor at the church. She and I drifted apart as close friends for obvious reasons. We were both going in different directions. She stayed on the narrow path and was into her Bible, and I was back on the wide path in the world with more compatible friends. My mother expressed her disappointment about her family's decision to turn back, but once again, I turned a stiff neck and a rebellious ear to her pleas.

In Matthew 7:13–14,

> Come to God through the narrow gate, because the wide gate and broad path is the way that leads to destruction-nearly everyone chooses that crowded road! The narrow gate and the difficult way leads to eternal life, so few even find it.

No Time to Kill

Come, my child, come while there's still time
I've called you so often oh child of mine
But off you go to do what you will
No time for me, only time to kill
Up on a mountain, you know me not
But I was there in the valley, or have you forgotten?
This world and its pleasures leave nothing to gain
Still on you go searching with an empty heart in vain
Many times, you cried out with your head in your hands
Did I not say, "Turn around, child, for here I stand?"
There is so little time that is left on the clock
I stand at the door, on and on I knock
Soon darkness will come with gloom and despair
Then you will turn but won't find me there
My child, I keep calling, but you still refuse to listen
You will end up in hell in your fallen condition
I love you, my child, and have given you grace
Turn around, my child, and seek my face
Look up! Look up! As you approach the last hour
For "I am" the "I am" the one and only true power
Remember, my child, I love you and always will
So do not harden your heart, for there is no time to kill.

9

From the Frying Pan and into the Fire

As I approached the age of fifteen, my rebellion was becoming more apparent. Coupled with that rebellion was a growing resentment for my father's authority and the constant lack of never having the needed school materials. I was past the point of frustration, and it was contributing to my poor attitude where my education was concerned. My teachers never ceased to put me at the center of attention when asked why I didn't have the necessary materials. I had hoped in vain that at some point, they were able to read between the lines and realize my parents were penniless. Or at the very least, ask me in private.

One day, my gym teacher asked me in front of the class, of course, why I wasn't dressed in my gym uniform. Again, not wanting to be embarrassed or humiliated, I responded by saying, "Because I didn't want to!" My response infuriated my gym teacher, and she angrily yelled at me to "get the h—— out of my class!" Then she spitefully reported me to the principal's office and said I was skipping her class! My answer to this dilemma was to find a way for this fifteen-year-old to quit school. I had zero desire to stay in school.

I told my mother that I didn't want to go back, but she insisted I was going to finish school whether I liked it or not! It was fairly obvious I didn't like it. I argued my point with her about how unfair it was for her to expect me to go without my daily school necessities. The truth of the matter was that I wasn't old enough to drop out of school. You had to be sixteen with written consent from a parent, and that's what my mother focused on. Mom stood firm, which frustrated me even more! I was determined to find a way to follow through with my plan.

I put a plan in action the next morning and began to intentionally miss the school bus. Mom quickly caught on to what I was doing and committed herself to drive me to school if that's what it took! What she didn't know was as she watched me enter the front door of the school, I would slip out the back and skip the whole day. I accomplished my mission without being detected by any school personnel. Rebellious? Ever so slightly. I did have a twinge of guilt knowing my mother's efforts were fruitless.

There were days Mom simply didn't have the gas or the money for the gas to take me to school, and that guaranteed me a day at home. Mom never failed to lecture me about how I would one day regret not getting a proper education, but her warning fell on deaf ears.

Dad always came home for his daily lunch break, and I made sure to hide upstairs until he left to return to work. I couldn't argue with him and get away with it as I did Mom. I finally exhausted my mother's efforts when it came to her taking me to school. Again, she told me I would suffer the consequences of not getting a high school diploma. YES! I gleefully won this battle! I still had a few months before turning sixteen, but I figured the school had given up on me coming back since I had already missed one hundred nineteen days of school. I was confident I was home free, and my school blues were over; that is, until one day, a truant officer showed up at the front door!

He was quite intimidating looking at six foot six. When Mom answered the door, he introduced himself and politely asked why I hadn't been attending school. She didn't spare me! I have tried and tried to get her to go, but she refuses. That was pretty much the truth. Then the truant officer informed my mother and me that I had to be sixteen with my parents' consent to quit school. Not what I wanted to hear, but I also knew I didn't want to face a judge for being incorrigible. UGH! I had to return to school!

With a hundred and nineteen absent days under my belt, I knew I wouldn't be promoted, so it made it even worse having to go back! The next morning, I caught the bus and grudgingly returned to school. The truant officer made it his mission to check and make sure I was in classes. There was no exhausting his efforts. I felt like I was in prison. My mother knew all too well how determined I was to quit, and when the time came for me to turn sixteen, she legally signed me out of school for good.

I felt liberated and vindicated. It was my first step in taking control of my life! I was your typical know-it-all teenager who was destined for a rude awakening called life! In the meantime, I was basking in my newfound freedom though limited. I still had to live under Dad's authoritative rule, and I wouldn't be turning eighteen for two years, and that was just too long to wait! I had to find a way out from under his tyranny. Until that moment became a reality, I made it my goal to avoid my dad by staying out as late as possible with friends. Most of the time, Dad was already in bed by the time I got home.

A few short months later, one of my cousins introduced me to a guy named John who was eighteen. We hit it off and started dating. In the early stages of seeing each other, John made it clear he wanted a steady relationship, which I was agreeable to. Five months into our relationship, John asked me to marry him. I thought he was kidding and laughed. Then I realized he was serious. At sixteen years old, I couldn't even begin to process his proposal! There was no way I was ready for marriage (that's an understatement). Then John said something that intrigued me. "You do know that if you marry me, you become a legal adult, and your father can't tell you what to do anymore."

He had a valid point I thought, *and I wouldn't have to wait until I was eighteen.* John's proposal was sounding more attractive by the minute; it was the quick fix I had been looking for, my free ticket out! I was getting fluent at making disastrous decisions!

Because I was underage, my mother had to sign a legal document permitting me to marry John, which she agreed to do. When it came to me, Mom chose the least path of resistance. John and I were married in Upper Marlboro, Maryland, courthouse, on March 7,

1975. I walked out of the courthouse free from my father's authority, but now legally bound to a man who would prove to be a controlling abuser! We stayed with my parents for a while until John suggested we move to Florida where his mother lived.

Before moving, I discovered I was pregnant. Mom was ecstatic upon hearing the news she was going to be a grandmother but disheartened at the same time John and I planned to move so far away. Honestly, I was uncomfortable putting that much distance between me and my family, but John convinced me the grass was greener there.

When we arrived in Florida, I instinctively knew it wasn't my home. I felt isolated, alone, and homesick for the place I originally wanted to escape. I immediately wanted to go back to Maryland. My consequential choices were becoming a cold reality check that had only just begun. I kept my insecurities to myself for the moment, not letting John know how I felt. I figured I would at least give my new surroundings a chance.

My new mother-in-law promptly laid down her rules, the key rule being if we were to stay with her, I had to have an abortion! In a very heated exchange, John told his mother, "That's not going to happen!" Our decision to keep our child didn't sit well with her, and she said we could not stay with her. His mother had the foreknowledge of the pregnancy before we moved, so I failed to understand why his mother didn't make her rules known to us while still in Maryland. I can only speculate she may have thought it was going to take a face-to-face confrontation, but even in her attempt to convince us it was for the better, her argument wasn't an option. It was very clear she didn't share in our baby's joy!

I wasn't about to let a golden opportunity go to waste, so I said, "John, let us go back to Maryland!" With no other available alternative, it was an effortless task to convince John; and with that settled, we made a *U*-turn and headed back north. Mom was elated to hear we were on our way back and to know she wouldn't miss the birth of her first grandchild. John got a job at the lumber company where my father worked, and we were able to move into an apartment of our own.

Our first child, John, aptly named after his father, was born on October 22, 1975. I became a first-time mother at the age of seventeen. Life was changing quickly for me—too quickly! I was becoming more aware with each passing day that quick fixes seldom work out in your favor.

I began to notice some negative characteristics about my new husband. When it came to work, he was extremely unreliable. He habitually missed work and would either get fired or quit on his own. The lumber company hired him back three times, and that was inclusive of me pleading with them one of those times to hire him back! With John unemployed, we were unable to keep the apartment, and we moved back in with my parents. John had become controlling and physically abusive, especially when nobody was around to witness his behavior. I had grown to be very afraid of him, and he used that fear to dominate me. I felt I had no identity or quality of life since everything I did or said was focused on pacifying John.

I kept these things hidden from Mom because I didn't want her to worry, but in due time, I did confide in her. As expected, she was genuinely concerned about my welfare. I was determined to make our marriage work based on a false hope John would change for the good one day. What I had yet to conclude was that it takes two to make a marriage work.

Whenever a financial crisis arose, and it did many times due to John walking away from employment, his remedy was to pack up our clothes and head back to Florida again. It was a trivial matter for him to leave behind an apartment full of furniture. Every time we moved into another home, I couldn't help but wonder how long it would be until we were forced to move again. It became a perpetual cycle for years to come.

Arriving in Florida with the clothes on our backs, John's mother, Barbara, agreed to let us stay with her until we could financially get a home of our own. I became pregnant with our second child soon after the move. This time, it was John and his mom who weren't happy about the news! He demanded I terminate the pregnancy, but I refused. He became very angry and became physically abusive. With a black eye and other bodily bruises, I called my mom who came to my rescue. She purchased a bus ticket for me, and I was on my way back to Maryland with my infant son. The trip took twenty-seven hours, which made it difficult traveling that long with a baby, but I was desperate to get out of my hellish situation. I was in survival mode!

My brother Jerry and his wife offered me a place to stay. Three months later, John traveled back to Maryland and begged me for mercy. With an apology and a promise that things would be better, I conceded to let him back in my life. I held onto the hope that his words were sincere. Our baby girl, Bobbie, was born on December 9, 1977. In less than two years after Bobbie's birth, I would conceive two more times. Just like before, John demanded I terminate the pregnancies; and this time, I followed through.

I would like to take a moment here to tell you, the reader, that if you have been through an abortion(s) and are feeling guilt, shame, and are having a hard time forgiving yourself, God will forgive you and heal you of the trauma if you ask Him. Years after my abortions, I was wracked with guilt and shame for what I had done to my children. I grieved over them! I couldn't forgive myself until I surrendered it to God, and He let me know He had forgiven me and that I needed to forgive myself. He also let me know my children are with Him and that when I get to heaven one day, I will get to meet them!

Taking a child's life is never justified in God's sight, but there is forgiveness for a repentant heart. Many years later, God revealed something very revelatory to me about abortion. One morning, as I was in my daily prayer time, in my mind's eye, God showed me an acorn and asked, "WHAT DO YOU SEE?"

Knowing I was looking at a seed, I replied, "An oak tree, Lord."

He then said, "I SEE A WHOLE FOREST! WHEN A CHILD IS ABORTED, NOT ONLY IS THAT CHILD'S LIFE TAKEN, BUT ALSO EVERY GENERATION THAT WOULD HAVE COME FROM THAT CHILD!"

I was astounded! Never before had I ever considered such truth! I am thankful God is boundless in His love and mercy! In PSALM 86:5, "FOR YOU, O LORD, ARE GOOD AND FORGIVING, ABOUNDING IN STEADFAST LOVE TO ALL WHO CALL UPON YOU."

John walked away from his job and his promises yet again, and we found ourselves living back in Florida with his mother! For John, it was about escaping responsibility and commitment. By this time in our unstable marriage, I had come to the disheartening conclusion that this was as good as it was going to get with John! Expecting him to keep a job and a place to call home would never be long term, but rather, how long would it be before we were forced to move!

John's temperament remained unpredictable so I kept the children out of his way as much as possible. My parents still had no phone, but Mom would stay in touch with me by calling from my grandmothers. During one of her welfare calls, I held back very little where John was concerned. She was naturally filled with anxiety for our safety. I told her I was reaching a crossroads in my marriage and wanted out from under the tyranny. Mom encouraged me to leave John for good, which I was on board with. I just didn't know how to financially make it happen yet.

John frequently went into violent acts of rage for the least provocation. Sometimes it was something as trivial as spilling a small amount of his morning coffee that would send him into a tirade. These outbursts entailed throwing furniture, punching holes in walls, and breaking glass! The kids and I lived in constant fear and turmoil. John was like a powder keg that kept the three of us walking around on dangerous landmines. I had to find a way out to break free and get the kids and me away from John's abuse!

With some financial help from my mother, I put a plan in motion. The kids and I were finally getting out of the abusive prison, and I was excited. I had a car that was in decent mechanical shape, which was a plus. After John went to work the next morning, I packed up our clothes and loaded our things in the car. I left Florida on my first full tank of gas and with high hopes and dreams for a new beginning. I felt the suffocating restraints of control and abuse begin to fall off with each passing mile, and it was pure freedom! The kids and I could breathe normally again!

The seventeen-hour trip back to Maryland went smoothly without any mechanical mishaps along the way. While I was living in Florida, my parents divorced, but they maintained a platonic and caring relationship. My father continued to take care of my mom although they both lived separately. They no longer lived in Beltsville but lived in a small city called Laurel six miles north. My father lived in a basement apartment, and my brother Jerry and his wife Liz lived in the upstairs part of the home. My mother lived in a low-income townhouse that was located within four miles of where my dad and brother lived. Dad helped Mom out financially with the monthly rent. Upon arriving in my home state, I was excited about embarking on a new chapter in my life. The kids and I moved into the townhome with Mom. She was relieved to see us back home, and so was I!

I knew I had the task ahead of me to locate employment, so once we got settled, I began my search. I informed my dad that I would take the responsibility of paying the monthly rent as soon as I became employed. Being a young mother with two small children to raise on my own was going to be a challenge but one that I was willing to face head-on! I successfully found a job in Beltsville and was able to start right away. Mom agreed to watch the kids while I worked, which saved me the added expense of daycare. Everything was falling perfectly in place! With my newfound determination and unshakeable confidence, I felt unstoppable! Things were finally coming together for the kids and me, but in the not-so-distant future, tragedy was about to strike at the heart of our family in a very unexpected and devastating way!

10

Crashing Down

My new life, as I like to call it, was going smoothly; and I remained optimistic about the future for the three of us. My mother was catching up on some quality time with her grandchildren and enjoying every minute of it. After getting off work one afternoon, I decided to drive over to Jerry and Liz's for a quick visit. When I arrived, Liz was busy preparing dinner. I sat at the kitchen table and chatted with her as she cooked. It was at the end of April, and the weather was warm enough to have the front door open, allowing fresh spring air to flow through the screen.

As I chatted with Liz, I suddenly heard my father's angry voice coming through the vent on the floor of the basement apartment. My youngest sister, Millie, and my three younger brothers, Terry, Eugene, and Alvin, lived with my father although Eugene, at the time, was in a disciplinary camp that was located two hours away. Alvin had recently been released from another local boy's reformatory and placed on probation. They both had gotten into some minor trouble, and their faces had come before the court system one too many times!

Alvin stated many times after being released that he hated the reformatory and would never go back! I was hoping he would follow through on his statement. As I heard Dad yelling, it sounded like he was in a rage, and I knew Alvin was on the receiving end. My father had come home from work to discover Alvin failing to do the chores

Dad outlined for him. I couldn't hear any responses from my brother as Dad demanded a reason as to why he hadn't done them.

I winced as I heard my father angrily threaten to call Alvin's probation officer. I felt compassion for my brother at that moment. Dad's verbal attack was violent. Within a few minutes, Alvin walked up the front steps to the house and entered through the screen door. Without saying a word to anyone, he sat down at the table opposite where I was sitting. I looked across the table at him and could visibly see the aftereffects that my father's raging words had on him.

He was very dejected as he sat there staring down at the floor. His girlfriend, Paula, pulled up outside and parked. Alvin abruptly got up and met her at the screen door and said, "Let's go!" With a surprised look on her face, Paula replied, "Go where? I just got here!"

"I don't care where! I just want to go," he replied!

As I watched them both leave in Paula's car, I knew Alvin wanted to escape his frustration even if only for a while. I left soon thereafter and made my way home. I had an alarm clock that was set for an early morning wake-up call for work.

The next morning as I left for work, the weather was chilly with light rain. It was in stark contrast to the beautiful, warm day before but typical for transitioning into spring. When I arrived at work, my supervisor directed me to my workstation for the day. I had been working at my station for a brief time when my supervisor approached me and said, "Sue, you have a phone call." The company had a phone that was centrally located in the work area of the factory for employee use. As I walked over to the phone, I thought it was odd that someone would be calling me this early in the morning. I was at a loss at who it could be since Mom and I didn't have a phone yet.

I picked up the receiver. "Hello!"

"Sue, get a hold of yourself!"

I instantly recognized the voice of my sister-in-law Liz. Her voice trembled as she continued to speak, "I have some bad news. Alvin is dead!"

I dropped the receiver and screamed, "No!"

My supervisor and coworkers came running toward me as I continued to scream! "Sue, what's wrong?"

I was too distraught to speak. My supervisor picked up the receiver I had dropped and found that Liz was still on the line. Liz informed her that she still needed to speak with me, and my supervisor slowly handed me the phone. It was then that Liz told me Alvin had committed suicide by hanging himself! I was devastated. Knowing he wanted to die made his death all the more painfully tragic! What a nightmare! I couldn't believe this was happening! It was April 30, 1980. Alvin had just celebrated his sixteenth birthday on April 1. My thoughtful coworkers tried comforting me, but I was inconsolable. I needed to be with my family! A close friend at work offered to drive me to Laurel, knowing I was too upset to drive myself. I couldn't believe a broken heart could hurt this much, but it was excruciating! My baby brother was gone!

I began to think about the night before as my friend drove me to Laurel. Alvin had been right across the table from me just hours before, *Why didn't I reach out to him? Why didn't I try to talk with him! Too late*, I thought! I recalled a brief conversation that took place three weeks earlier between Alvin and my mother. Paula and Alvin came by for a visit. Mom was aware that Alvin was violating some of his probation rules since being released from the reformatory and cautiously reminded him that if he continued to jeopardize the court order, he ran the risk of being sent back to the reformatory. His response was chilling! "Before I go back to that place, I will hang myself!"

I looked at him and said, "Stop being so dramatic, Alvin," not believing for a second he was serious about what he had said. Now, those haunting words chill me to the bone! Never in a million years did I think he would follow through on such a threat! Yet here I was, facing the cold, hard reality of that fulfilled threat!

What was the final straw for him? What pushed him over the edge? I thought of my father's threat the night before to call Alvin's probation officer. Was that the tipping point? Did he die thinking nobody loved him? Oh, God, I wanted desperately to turn back the hands of time to have that needed conversation with him, but most of all, to tell him how much I love him. It grieved me to realize now how much silent pain and torment he must have been going through!

When I arrived at Jerry's, the scene I encountered was not what I expected. There were multiple police cars and a coroner's vehicle parked on the street in front of the house. I had wrongfully assumed the process of removing my brother's body from the premises had already occurred, but the police and medical examiner were still going through their protocol of the investigation. It was too much to process! It looked like a crime scene. In a spiritual sense, it was because Satan, the liar, was successful in convincing my brother that death was his only option in escaping the frustrations of life and attaining peace, but God's word says in JOHN 10:10, "THE THIEF (SATAN) COMES TO STEAL, KILL, AND DESTROY." In that same verse, Jesus gives us His loving truth that is based on better promises. "I HAVE COME THAT THEY [everyone] MAY HAVE LIFE, AND HAVE IT TO THE FULL."

That is God's will for your life—to have it to the full! Jesus also tells us in JOHN 8:44, "WHEN HE [SATAN] LIES, HE SPEAKS HIS NATIVE LANGUAGE, FOR HE IS A LIAR AND THE FATHER OF LIES." If you have ever considered suicide as a viable option for any reason, know with assurance that it's the enemy of your soul whispering the same deadly lies he whispered in my brother's ear. Many have said that suicide is a permanent solution to a temporary problem, and that statement has a lot of validity; but in saying that, please understand I am not minimizing the issues you may have gone through or are presently going through.

What I would like to emphatically tell you is that there is love, hope, and genuine peace in Jesus Christ who is waiting for you to surrender your life to Him! He has an excellent fail-proof plan for your life that has yet to unfold.

In Jeremiah 29:11, "FOR I KNOW THE PLANS I HAVE FOR YOU, DECLARES THE LORD, PLANS TO PROSPER YOU AND NOT TO HARM YOU, PLANS TO GIVE YOU A HOPE AND A FUTURE." These are the promises not even the finest universities can back with a guarantee. One more thing before moving on, God's love for you is unconditional and everlasting. It has no expiration date! You may not like the person you see in the mirror, but God says you're a beautiful work, His very own priceless masterpiece. Nothing and no one can ever separate you from His love.

In Romans 8:35, "Can anything ever separate us from Christ's love? does it mean he no longer loves us if we have trouble or calamity, or are persecuted, or are hungry, or destitute, or are in danger, or threatened with death?" The answer is a resounding "No!" There is always hope in Christ.

The grim scenario I was beholding only confirmed the bone-chilling reality that it wasn't a nightmare. My youngest brother was dead! I couldn't bear the thought of knowing that his body was still on the premises. For a brief moment, I thought how appropriate and befitting the weather was for such a tragedy! The cold, damp air sent a chill through my body. I slowly stepped from the car and began to make my somber walk through the yard and up to the front steps where Jerry lived.

I was midway through the yard when Jerry suddenly charged out of the front door and ran toward me. He was crying as he quickly threw the arm of his jacket over my head and said, "Sue! Don't look. He's still hanging there!" I had been so focused on getting to the front door that I never perceived that Alvin was still hanging from a tree just twenty-five feet to my right! I desperately wanted to break free from Jerry and run to my baby brother. I wanted to embrace him and tell him how much I loved him, to never let go! But it was too late; he was gone.

Spring had arrived, and the birds were singing, but I was unable to hear them.

Masterpiece

I see you there, and you're about to break
I know your thoughts, but you're not a mistake!
Your heart is so broken, beaten, and shattered
You think no one cares, and your life doesn't matter

You feel helpless and hopeless embittered and scorned
Many times, you have wondered, *Why was I born?*
Your wounds are many, but you keep them concealed
You have no real hope to ever be healed
You dwell in the past with all its regrets

Constant reminders Satan won't let you forget
Depression and sorrow have taken your joy
The thief comes to steal, kill, and destroy

You're surrounded by DARKNESS, but you cry out for light
Then Satan whispers just take your life!

True to his nature, he lies once again!
He says your peace will be waiting; it will be at the end.

But I am the way, the truth, and the life
Come unto me, for I am the light

My love for you is faithful and true
Turn now to me, and I will make you brand-new.
I will heal all your wounds hiding within
My plans for you are yes and amen.

I crafted you as my masterpiece
From the top of your head to the soles of your feet.

Your decision will determine the path that you take
Remember, I love you, you're not a mistake

IN EPHESIANS 2:10, "FOR WE ARE GOD'S MASTERPIECE. HE HAS CREATED US ANEW IN CHRIST JESUS, SO WE CAN DO THE GOOD THINGS HE PLANNED FOR US LONG AGO."

11

Moving Forward

As Jerry and I entered the house, I was met by several grieving faces of family members. My brother Terry and I embraced as we wept. No words were necessary as we shared our mutual sorrow. I thought of my brother Eugene with a heavy heart because he wasn't there and would never get another opportunity to see Alvin alive. The disciplinary camp where he was held decided to release him early given the sudden tragic circumstances and the impending funeral.

I walked to the kitchen area and glanced at the table where Alvin and I had sat the night before, not knowing that mere hours later, he would be gone, and our family would be mourning! It was all very surreal! He was just here last night! I turned to see my father standing alone, leaning against the kitchen counter. He looked at me as tears streamed down his face and said, "My son, my son. He's gone!" He was so broken! His demeanor reminded me of the revival night at the church in Beltsville when he gave his life to Christ. I felt overwhelming compassion for my father because of his grief-stricken state! I thought of the raging words he had spent on Alvin the night before and how the guilt he was feeling had to be weighing heavily on him. I was previously told that my father was the first one to discover my brother's body when he prepared to leave for work that morning. Dad looked at me again. "I will never forget the look on his face. He cried!"

As the news of Alvin's death began to spread that morning, many of his friends came by to give their condolences. Such was the case for our family, Alvin's friends were shocked to discover he would take his life! At this point, my mother was home watching my children and had yet to be informed of my brother's death. My aunt Mildred, Mom's older sister, arrived when she heard about the devastating news. She knew all too well how difficult it was going to be telling Mom.

Telling a mother that she has lost a child is something she never wants to hear, but Mom had to be told regardless. Aunt Mildred volunteered to tell Mom, which took the burden off of my shoulders and my siblings. On the ride to the townhome, all I could think about was the heavy toll the news would have on Mom. I was dreading it!

We arrived and walked down the sidewalk and up to the front door. I didn't have the door key with me, so my aunt knocked on the door. She quickly turned to us and said, "I know this is going to be hard, but you have to be strong for your mother."

I couldn't speak for my siblings, but it was going to be impossible for me! Mom answered the door and was initially surprised to see her sister there with the rest of us. Her smile quickly faded when I burst out sobbing. My heart was breaking for her!

"What's wrong, Mildred?" Mom asked as she searched my aunt's face.

By this time, my aunt was crying too as she led my mother to sit down on the couch. "Jeanie, it's Alvin," my aunt began.

Mom looked at her. "No! Don't tell me."

Aunt Mildred painfully continued, "Jeanie, he's dead!"

Mom let out a blood-curdling scream that came from deep within her soul! The anguish that was known only to a mother. It got worse! Assuming Alvin had died in a car accident, Mom asked my aunt through tears, "Whose car was he in?"

There was an uncomfortable silence as Mom looked to one face and then another for an answer to her question. I couldn't stand the hesitation any longer, but I also knew that what I was going to tell her would twist the knife that was already embedded in her heart. "Mama, he hung himself!"

She screamed again as my aunt tried comforting her, but Mom was inconsolable.

My sister-in-law Liz initiated the necessary funeral plans. The funeral home strongly recommended a closed casket due to the disfigurement from the hanging, but my mother adamantly rejected their advice and firmly stated that she wanted to see her son before the burial. The rest of our family was not on board with Mom's request. The service would be difficult enough, but we held our opinions, and the funeral home respectfully moved forward with my mother's wishes.

Stepping inside the funeral home was the second hardest thing I have ever had to do; the first one was looking at my brother in his casket! I can bear witness by stating here that his casket should have been closed! Eugene stayed in an adjoining room. He wanted no part in viewing Alvin, and I didn't blame him. I would have preferred the same, but I felt obligated to stay by my mother's side.

In the days following the funeral, our family was parked in the raw and emotional upheaval of losing my brother. It was going to be challenging to try and find a new level of normal without him. The thought of having to do life from here on out without Alvin was heart-rending! What does that look like? How do you even begin? It seemed unattainable!

My mother had become very withdrawn and depressed. In the coming weeks, she had come dangerously close to a nervous breakdown, which had us all concerned. Nothing could be more painfully consuming than a broken and grieving heart. The only person who can touch that kind of pain is Jesus. Psalm 147:3 tells us, "He heals up the brokenhearted and binds up their wounds." A broken heart is a wounded heart, but Jesus heals!

I was thankful my father was there for Mom during her greatest time of need and helped her cope with the tragic event. Dad dealt with his grief the only way he knew how. He escaped to his sanctuary, his shed! He poured himself into a project that promised to take his mind off the devastation even if only for a while. My dreams of starting a new life for myself and my children were short-lived. Mom could no longer watch the kids while I worked since her mental well-being had become unstable. She needed her space and time to heal. Having no money coming in, I had to give up my home! I had run out of options and was back in survival mode.

John called me after hearing about Alvin and suggested that the kids and I move back to Florida. I felt I had gained so much ground, only to be brought back to ground zero! Having no plan B, I threw in the towel and reluctantly agreed to give our marriage one more chance. Like many times before, John promised things would be better. Somewhere from deep within me, there was a small flicker of hope that maybe, just maybe, he would follow through on his promise this time. Perhaps the enormity of the tragic event would compel John to be more compassionate and loving with me and his children. I had to hope for the best!

I hated the thought of leaving my family at such a vulnerable time, but I also felt that at this juncture, the change would be beneficial for my emotional healing process. The familiar surroundings that I loved had now become a constant, painful reminder of my brother's death. After moving back with John, the days and months were intermittent with waves of grief. Something would trigger a memory of Alvin and, without fail, left me weeping. One of his favorite movies was called *THE KING OF KINGS*. It came on every year around Easter, and he would put his life on hold ensuring to be home to watch it. I truly believe he was touched by the love of Christ while watching that movie. My heart ached just thinking about it. My memories and pictures were all I had left of him, and they had become more precious to me than gold!

Again, we stayed with John's mom until we were able to get a place of our own. It didn't take John long to fall back into his abusive pattern. I was confronted yet one more time with a broken promise. Whenever he would witness me going through a grieving moment, he would angrily yell at me and say he'd had enough of seeing me cry and that I needed to get over Alvin's death and move on with life! His harsh and unsympathetic statement was like a cold, hard slap in the face! I couldn't believe what I was hearing! He followed up that statement with, "Don't let me see you crying anymore!" Oh, that grief worked that way where you could turn it off at will! Unfortunately, it didn't; so whenever I became overcome with sorrow, I made sure to escape to the bathroom or another secluded place outside where John couldn't see me.

John became employed at a local lumber company, and I was able to get a job at a factory that was within walking distance from his mother's. The situation worked out well since we had one car. Neither job paid well, but they afforded us two incomes, which were enough to get into a place of our own. Housing was inexpensive in Florida compared to Maryland which made it easier to find an affordable rental. We moved into a two-bedroom duplex, but it put me twenty minutes from work. Thankfully, I had a coworker who lived less than a mile from our new home who was willing to pick me up and drop me off.

It felt somewhat liberating to be working and earning an income again. John insisted on handling the finances, and that required me to surrender my paycheck to him every week. Knowing how controlling he was made me nervous, not having any access to the checking account to verify where the money was going and never seeing one of his paychecks. He treated me like an outsider, which means it was none of my business! I knew John was buying drugs, and that's why he kept me in the dark about our finances because he didn't want me to know what he was spending on his habit! When I checked the mail, I saw that the bills were being neglected and were marked "past due!" Although I enjoyed my new job, I felt like I was working to pay for his drug habit, and it frustrated me! When he was forced to pay bills, he had no access to money for drugs, which sent him into one of his violent rages!

He was a madman! I couldn't go on expecting my kids or me to keep living in a toxic environment! I had to come up with another plan to get me and my children free from this man for good and break this cycle of abuse! There was no going back this time and no more broken promises. My marriage to John was over, but I had to come up with the finances to see my plan through. For now, I continued to walk around the landmines and take each day one at a time.

I eventually convinced my sister Millie and her boyfriend, Mark, to move to Florida. Millie instantly fell in love with Florida. Mark secured a job with me at the factory, and they found an apartment to rent. I was happy to at least have some of my family living in the same state. At the forefront of my thought process was to get out from under my volatile relationship with John. Then one day out of the blue, or so I thought, John casually approached me and suggested we separate.

I was excited and barely able to maintain my composure, I said, "Yes, I think that would be a good idea!" I felt as though I had just been handed a gift on a silver platter! After we separated with John leaving the duplex, I found out he was having an affair with a coworker. Being armed with this knowledge only solidified my resolve to end our marriage! As I thought of Dad's authority and how I had to get out from under his rulership, all I can say is, lesson learned, but with a lot of bumps and bruises along the way!

The kids and I stayed in the duplex until I was served an eviction notice! My income alone wouldn't pay the rent, and John refused to give me any financial support. The eviction process in Florida takes two weeks or less. I had to find a place and quickly! Mark and Millie offered their help by letting us stay with them, and I was grateful. It would do until I could locate something more accommodating for me and the kids. Millie didn't work so she blessed me with daycare.

Within a few weeks, I found a house for rent that was less than a mile from my work. I asked Millie and Mark if they would be willing to share the cost of renting the home, and they agreed. The proximity of the home to our jobs worked out well for Mark and me. Millie continued to provide the daycare I needed for John and Bobbie, and our new journey was in motion. Once again, I had a renewed optimism for the future. I knew with confidence there was no turning back! Mom was very relieved to hear the kids and I were no longer living under the constant threat of verbal and physical abuse. John had me served with divorce papers, and within a month, we were officially divorced. I could finally exhale!

12

No Turning Back

I continued making new friends among my colleagues at work. There was one employee in particular named Marc who I hadn't gotten an opportunity to meet and converse with yet. He was very quiet and shy and made little eye contact with anyone, which intrigued me. I was instantly attracted to him! I have heard it said that opposites attract; in this case, I would have to harmonize with that statement since I am very bold and outspoken! I learned from other coworkers that Marc was a widower with three young children. His wife had died in an accident six years prior. I was taken aback to hear something so traumatic. Upon hearing of his unfortunate tragedy, I began to see this man through the eyes of newfound respect and compassion. He had the weighty responsibility of raising his children without their mother, and that alone had to be a daunting task!

I thought about how his past trauma and how it may be playing a key role in his reluctance to talk with anyone. I was sure to keep my distance for the moment even though my secret desire was for an opportunity to talk and get acquainted with him.

Every year, our company held a picnic for their employees. I inquired in a roundabout way if Marc had planned to go, and to my delight, he was! The picnic would be my long-awaited chance to break the ice and get to know this man I had become attracted to. The only obstacle standing in my way was THE NERVE! I guess I am a little shy! The day of the picnic arrived along with a lot of anxiety and anticipation. My heart skipped a beat as I saw Marc pull up and park. I instinctively knew today was the day, and it was!

Later in the afternoon, I took advantage of a "now or never" moment to strike up a conversation with Marc. As we both made small talk, the tension faded, and we became more relaxed with each other in our conversation. When I felt the timing was right, I revealed the secret attraction I had for him in my heart and then held my breath until he responded. He responded with a warm smile, and he let me know the attraction was mutual.

We started dating, and I discovered a very thoughtful, loving, and compassionate person behind all that shyness. A man who was genuine and transparent! When I considered all of his positive character traits, I was confident I had found a winner! After three months of dating, Marc asked me to marry him. His exact words were, "Woman, I'm stoned crazy, head over heels in love with you. Will you marry me?" I was flabbergasted! His proposal flattered me, but I was fearful at the same time. Despite all of Marc's positive attributes, I was hesitant! I believed the mixed bag of emotions I was experiencing were stemming from the negative side effects of my marriage to John. My relationship with John was the only template I had with which to gauge a marriage.

Although Marc never gave me any indication or reason to believe he would be abusive, I was still uncertain. Marc was understanding and willing to wait and give me more time to heal. Over the span of a year, all of my apprehension vanished, and we were married without ever looking back! Like I stated, "He's a winner," and hasn't deviated from that title! We had now become a combined family of nine! Marc's oldest child, Pam, was ten years old; then David, seven; and lastly, Scott, five. Our children were all close in age with John being eight and Bobbie being five. Although our newly formed family wasn't without its challenges, with time, we progressed with maturity and, most of all, love.

One obstacle we often faced as a larger family was finding rental properties that were willing to rent to a family the size of ours. We were turned away numerous times, and it had become a frustrating issue! We managed to find a couple of properties that were willing to give us a lease, but the homes lacked the room or other needed essentials. We couldn't afford to be too picky, so we made the homes work for a while. Eventually, Marc and I decided to buy a home to get what we needed. I wasn't fond of the idea of purchasing a home in Florida because I still desired to, one day, move back home to Maryland.

Like me, Marc wasn't a native Floridian. He was born and raised in Columbus, Ohio. We often talked about the possibility of moving back north in the future. Although my sister lived close by, my yearning to go back home never dwindled. Florida lacked the seasonal changes that Marc and I both grew up loving. I'm not a fan of multiple blizzards in a single winter season, but I could appreciate one good snowfall a year! I felt our children were missing out on the seasonal activities as well such as sledding and simply building a snowman. The beauty of autumn can never be overstated! Oddly enough, our kids rarely wanted to play outside and spent most of their activity time indoors while living in Florida. They complained that it was too hot to be out, and I was proned to agree! For the moment, our dream of moving north was put on hold.

Marc was offered a new job at a cabinet company as an installer, and with that offer came the potential to make good money. His income potential would be based on each cabinet installation. The new opportunity looked very promising, and we were extremely excited! Any increase in our income was always welcomed with our family size, especially the grocery bill! With three growing boys, their appetites only increased with every growth spurt. The excitement turned out to be short-lived. Not long after Marc started working in his new position, the company's installations started drying up. Our financial hope of getting ahead ended in bitter disappointment! Marc was well-liked by his new employer, and he was offered another position within the warehouse building the cabinets.

Marc enjoyed his new line of work, and the hourly wage gave us a more secure income. After working in the warehouse for about six months, the company began to struggle financially for a second time; and as a result, Marc's hours were reduced. Not what we wanted to hear! Adding to the hardship, Marc was preparing to leave for work one morning and discovered our van had been stolen! The police recovered it two days later, and it was in a disgusting mess! It appeared the thieves used the van to haul stolen car parts, which left huge grease stains on the seats. The ignition was busted and hanging. Marc had to start the van with a screwdriver to get it home. Ironically the same key the thieves used to steal it!

The pay cut Marc took was soon evidenced in our mounting bills. They were delinquent, and we were faced with some critical decisions. To try and save what was left of our credit, we resolved to sell our home and move to Marc's home state of Ohio. As much as I desired to return to my home state, the housing in Ohio was half the cost. It was the wiser choice for our family, or so I thought! We would need at least a four-bedroom home. Millie was disheartened when I told her our plans. I had some guilt over the distance I was putting between her and me, but I assured her no amount of distance could ever separate our hearts or my love for her although my heart was breaking to leave her.

We needed the house to sell as in yesterday to keep our heads above water! Thankfully, it did! With our home sold and the moving truck packed, we were on our way to Columbus. Mom was a little disappointed we were moving to Ohio instead of Maryland, but I told her it was only a seven-hour drive between us, and I promised her I would visit often. Since leaving Maryland the last time, my father had moved from the basement apartment and purchased a two bedroom mobile home that was located in a mobile home park in Laurel. He and Mom shared the home. Although their relationship remained platonic, Dad continued to take care of her, and I was very grateful that he did. I never quite understood why my parents divorced after many years of marriage, but I do believe the tragic events of my brother's death brought them closer together.

Carol lived close by in another park located across the street from my parents and would stop by often to see how they were doing, and I took comfort in knowing that. Within a few days of our arrival in Ohio, we were able to find a four-bedroom home in a nice family-oriented neighborhood. The monthly rent was more than reasonable, but if I had done more thorough research before the move,

I would have realized the wages in Ohio we're considerably lower! Disappointingly lower! Regardless, we were here and ready to dig our heels in, and there was no turning back. Our move was made in July, and the kids still had some summer fun before starting school.

When the season transitioned into early fall, it was a welcome change. The colors of the autumn foliage were beautiful to behold! I knew without a doubt that this was one of the seasons I missed the most while living in Florida. Marc and I made as many financial adjustments as possible to accommodate our lower incomes. I shopped for the cheapest grocery stores I could find! We still had some extra cash from the sale of our home, but it was vanishing rapidly! Before long, the winter season was upon us, and we were looking forward to our first snowfall.

The Ohio winter didn't disappoint us! The kids were ecstatic to see the snowfall. Keeping them inside was not an option no matter how cold! On a comparative level, getting them outdoors in Florida was completely the opposite!

I found employment nearby at a lab where you were trained to wire very small pressure cells for the government. The wiring process was done under a microscope with a set of tweezers. If the cells were wired incorrectly, the cell had the potential to shoot through the ceiling when being tested in the next department. I was informed during my interview that this mishap had taken place a few times in the past, and therefore, I needed to be extremely attentive when it came to the wiring process. No pressure, right? Pardon the pun!

The training would take an average of six months before a trainee would be making the company a profit; however, after four months, I had successfully achieved that goal and was given a pay raise for my efforts. I continued to meet every challenge and excelled in my new position. Then one day, a coworker whose workstation was next to mine came to work visibly sick! She was very pale with a horrible, croupy cough and admitted to having a fever! When she was asked by another worker why she didn't stay home, she replied, "I can't afford to miss any work!" I could sympathize with her sentiment being under a financial strain myself, but at the same time, I couldn't afford to miss work either! I couldn't help but be concerned when considering how contagious her illness may be.

She lasted a couple of hours before succumbing to her illness and was forced to go home. My contagious concerns were fully realized two days later when I became sick with the same symptoms! I developed a high fever and a painful cough that made me feel like my chest would explode! I was incredibly weak and stayed in bed. I don't think I had ever been that sick in my life! After three days with no improvement, Marc took me to see a doctor. The doctor said I was on the verge of bronchial pneumonia! I was sent home with medicine and ordered to stay in bed and continue to rest.

I returned to work seven days later still feeling somewhat weak. Nevertheless, I couldn't afford to miss any more time from work. The days I missed promised to set us back financially. I was still in my probationary period at work, which made me ineligible for any type of sick leave. My first phone call was to the rental office. I explained to them the details of our recent hardship and that the rent would be a week late, but they were less than sympathetic! In fact, they proceeded to inform me that because I was paying the rent late, I would also need to pay the following month's rent in advance as well! I tried reasoning with them about the impossibility of that happening, but they weren't budging!

I hung up the phone feeling exceedingly disheartened and at a loss of what to do! I felt like we were between a rock and a hard place! We had most of the rent that was presently due; we just needed one more week without the requirement for the extra month's rent! When Marc got home from work, I shared the predicament we were in concerning the rent. After a moment of brooding silence, he asked, "How much money do we have in the bank?" I told him what we had, and he said, "We're moving to Maryland!"

I was shocked! Did I hear him correctly? I wasn't expecting that response at all! "Are you serious?"

"Yes! Let's start packing!"

The money we had was enough to move us. I immediately started packing before Marc had a chance to change his mind! Even though I hadn't been living my life for the Lord in recent years, I had been secretly praying He would make a way for us to move back to Maryland. I learned later on Mom was praying the same prayer. When I called to give her the news, she was over the moon! We're moving to Maryland! I'm going home!

13

God Is Faithful to Answer Prayer

When we prepared to leave Ohio, our oldest, Pam, who was seventeen, asked if she could stay in Ohio with her maternal grandmother. I was against her request and stood upon my conviction that our family should stay together and that she needed to move with us. But after some thoughtful consideration, Marc agreed to let her stay since she would be turning eighteen in a few short months, and she would be in good hands with her grandmother.

We acknowledged we would have to make some temporary sacrifices regarding our living arrangements once we arrived in Maryland. My parent's two-bedroom home wouldn't sufficiently hold our entire family, so my brother Jerry and his wife offered to keep John and David until we were able to get on our feet. Although it was temporary, and Marc and I were thankful for my brother's help, we wanted to get our family back under one roof as soon as possible! The rest of us stayed with my parents.

Even with John and David staying with my brother, we off-loaded our things in a storage facility after arriving in Maryland. Although John and David were staying at my brother's home, it was still a tight squeeze for the four of us in my parent's home. My mother graciously gave up her bedroom for Marc and me and slept on the couch. My parents were sacrificing a great deal to help us out, and we were grateful.

If you haven't already come to the startling conclusion yet, we had become quite fluent at moving, and the future still holds many more! Once we got settled, our top priority was seeking and securing employment. Marc and I had a few years of experience working in the cultured marble industry, which started in the company where we met in Florida, so we began to focus our search in that area. The only marble manufacturing plant we could locate was in a small suburb called White Plains, and it was over an hour away, an hour and fifteen minutes to be exact! It would mean a two-and-half-hour daily trip and a lot of wear and tear on our already high-mileage car. We did have a van, but it was repossessed not long after moving in with my parents. But we needed employment and a home for our family with all of us under one roof. Desperate times called for desperate measures, and we applied for a position.

With our previous experience, Marc and I were hired on the spot, which was exactly what we had hoped for. With both of us working together again, it worked out well economically since we only had one vehicle. After obtaining employment, I began my search for a home. It would prove to be a greater challenge now that our credit had taken some hard hits. With every application came a non-refundable application fee that began adding up with every refusal!

I determined to tell the leasing agents upfront about our credit issues before giving them another fee to avoid throwing away any more money! Just as I suspected, our credit wouldn't get Marc and me a lease. I was becoming increasingly frustrated by the day! People fell on hard times, but they still needed a place to live! Being in a valley has a way of renewing your faith, so I began to cry out to the Lord for His help. I was hoping for a microwave answer from Him, but my request seemed to be in the oven! I was on my knees daily even though the situation looked unchanging and hopeless. At times, I felt like my prayers weren't making it past the ceiling and thought about giving up. I was reminded of a parable in LUKE 18:1–8.

ONE DAY JESUS TOLD HIS DISCIPLES A STORY
TO SHOW THAT THEY SHOULD ALWAYS PRAY AND
NEVER GIVE UP. THERE WAS A JUDGE IN A CER-

TAIN CITY, HE SAYS, WHO NEITHER FEARED GOD NOR CARED ABOUT PEOPLE. A WIDOW OF THAT CITY CAME TO HIM REPEATEDLY, SAYING, GIVE ME JUSTICE IN THIS DISPUTE WITH MY ENEMY. THE JUDGE IGNORED HER FOR A WHILE, BUT FINALLY, HE SAID TO HIMSELF, I DON'T FEAR GOD OR CARE ABOUT PEOPLE, BUT THIS WOMAN IS DRIVING ME CRAZY. I'M GOING TO SEE THAT SHE GETS JUSTICE BECAUSE SHE IS WEARING ME OUT WITH HER CON-STANT REQUESTS. THEN THE LORD SAID, LEARN A LESSON FROM THIS UNJUST JUDGE. EVEN HE REN-DERED A JUST DECISION IN THE END. SO DON'T YOU THINK GOD WILL SURELY GIVE JUSTICE TO HIS CHOSEN PEOPLE WHO CRY OUT TO HIM DAY AND NIGHT? WILL HE KEEP PUTTING THEM OFF? I TELL YOU, HE WILL GRANT JUSTICE TO THEM QUICKLY.

Even though I wasn't looking for justice, the point Jesus was making was don't give up! I couldn't afford to throw in the towel, knowing my answer had to come from the Lord. For many of us, it's waiting in the hallway until the door opens that can be the most difficult part of our prayers! I felt as though we were stuck in neu-tral, but at the same time, reverse was not an option. God's timing is always perfect when we stand in faith and don't give up.

One afternoon Carol dropped by on her way home from work. After exchanging some small talk with Mom, Carol asked, "Are you ready to go?"

I was puzzled by her question. "Go where?"

She said, "I'm going to use my credit to cosign an apartment lease for you and Marc."

Did I hear her right? Yes! My prayers were going past the ceiling after all! Thank you, Lord! God used Carol in a big way to answer a desperate prayer, and I was so very grateful for her act of kindness. I was very relieved to be getting into a place of my own. We were moving forward. There's one thing in life I have learned, and that is

God never works in a way that you think He will. He always moves in ways you never expected. Don't try to figure it out; just let Him do the driving! He will never steer you wrong.

We settled into the apartment and were relieved to have our family under one roof again. A few months later, our high-mileage car said, "I quit!" A friend of Carol offered us an older car he had no use for. He informed us that the car was in working condition but couldn't guarantee for how long. He sold us the car for forty dollars! It was definitely worth the asking price even if it only lasted a month. It actually lasted six months! No complaining here, but, again, we were faced with the issue of needing a reliable car. Our budget wouldn't allow us to purchase one. Forty-dollar cars only came around once in a lifetime, at least the ones in working condition. I took my petition to the miracle maker because that's just what we needed, a miracle! Marc and I couldn't afford to miss work for any lengthy time. We had to have a microwave answer respectively.

My ex-mother-in-law Barbara would call from time to time to check in to see how Bobbie and John were doing. We remained friends after John and I divorced mainly because of her grandchildren. She happened to call the day after our car quit to see how everyone was getting along. I told her the children were doing well and briefly mentioned our transportation issue. The call ended with "Take care and talk to you soon."

Two days later, Barbara called to inform me that she had a car for us. The only thing needed was someone to come to Florida and drive the vehicle back to Maryland. She explained that the elderly woman she worked for could no longer drive her car and wanted to give it to us after Barbara told her about the dilemma we were in. The car had nineteen thousand miles on it, practically brand-new! I was in awe of God's goodness! In PHILIPPIANS 4:19, "AND MY GOD SHALL SUPPLY ALL YOUR NEEDS ACCORDING TO HIS RICHES AND GLORY IN CHRIST JESUS." In my journal, that gets recorded as a miracle.

My brother Terry offered to take a bus to Florida and drive the car back. God even supplied a driver! On the first day we drove our miracle car to work, a coworker remarked on how lucky we were, but

I quickly clarified his remark by telling him that luck had nothing to do with it, and that car was an answer to prayer.

I continued moving forward in my renewed faith-based journey and began searching for a Spirit-filled church. I found a place called "The Laurel Tabernacle." The teaching was exceptional and uncompromising and refreshing. It felt so wonderful to be back in the house of God and blessed to have a husband who desired to come with me. Things were progressing monetarily for us on our new job. Our experience allowed for favorable pay increases. We were finally pulling out of survival mode and able to exhale a bit. In a few months, I was promoted to plant manager, which was accompanied by another pay raise and a great deal of responsibility. I was up to the challenge, at least, most of it.

The biggest challenge I faced was being the only female employee who was now a supervisor to an all-male crew! It was slightly intimidating working with that much testosterone. Some of the employees could be taxing in more ways than one. Sometimes it didn't have anything to do with my management position but everything to do with my faith. I would often read my Bible on my morning breaks.

One morning as I was reading, an employee named Dan started making his way to where I was sitting. I knew from previous conversations with him about my faith that he was going to go derogatory on me! To be honest, Dan was very irritating and easily got under my skin, but I didn't want to respond to his confrontation negatively, so I prayed in that instant, "Holy Spirit! Give me the godly response to whatever Dan speaks."

Then, here he was, standing two feet in front of me and glaring down. "You think you're better than me, don't you?"

I looked up from my Bible. "Excuse me?" My reply was a stall tactic. I heard him the first time, but I hadn't heard the Holy Spirit yet.

He continued, "You think you're better than me because you read that Bible!"

Then, I didn't have to wait any longer, the Spirit spoke! I calmly looked Dan in the face and said, "If you feel condemned, it is by your own conscience, and not by me."

Without one single response, he turned and walked away from me. Thank you, Holy Spirit! I knew I couldn't trust my flesh to reply because the situation had great potential to become unpleasant. I may have wanted to call fire down from heaven and consume him! I was fully aware that Satan was using Dan to attack me.

God tells us in JAMES 4:7, "THEREFORE, SUBMIT TO GOD, RESIST THE DEVIL, AND HE WILL FLEE FROM YOU." I would like to say that was the last time the enemy used Dan to confront me, but he never gives up or takes a vacation! Satan is always looking for a more opportune time to launch another one of his missile attacks, but God is greater and will always send Satan fleeing if we submit to Him first. Remember, 1 JOHN 4:4, "GREATER IS HE THAT IS IN ME THAN HE THAT IS IN THE WORLD."

Although Marc started out working in the plant, the company began using him out in the field as an installer and a delivery man. My brother Terry was hired by the company and was used as Marc's helper whenever he did installations. Terry and his family came to stay with Marc and me for a while as they too were experiencing some financial difficulties. I could relate to having been there myself, and it was within my power to help. The only thing missing in our home was a dog, not really. But a coworker had some puppies he was trying to get rid of and guilted us into taking one. Living in a third-floor apartment wasn't an ideal space for a pup that showed promising signs of becoming a large dog! He was a mix between a Rottweiler and a Labrador, and we named him Samson.

We had lived in the apartment for a year and felt we were financially stable enough to start looking for a house to lease, preferably, in the Laurel area. I was looking forward to having a yard again for the kids and our growing dog. One day, as Marc and I were on our way to my parents, I spotted a vacant home. As we slowed to have a closer look, I saw an older gentleman exit the front door of the home, and we stopped to see if we could get some information. Just so happens he was the owner and said the house was a rental. We told the man that we were in the process of rebuilding our credit and that would he be willing to rent the home to us. He was agreeable to leasing the home to us, and he said he would waive the security deposit if we wanted to clean and paint the house.

We jumped on the offer! The prospect of having a yard again was something the whole family got excited about. We signed a one-year lease and started the cleaning process. The previous owners left the home in a disgusting mess, but we agreed to the terms, grabbed the bleach, and rolled up our sleeves. After a lot of sweat and elbow grease, our new residence looked and smelled much better! The basement was partially finished, which worked out well for Terry and his family until they became stable again. The extra space provided both families the needed privacy. We settled in comfortably and were satisfied, that is until we got the first water bill. It was a partial bill for only six weeks in the amount of $935.00! My initial thought was it had to be a clerical error! There was no possible way this bill was correct!

When I called the utility company to dispute the amount, they all-too-eagerly assured me the bill was indeed correct! I was shocked! The utility personnel said, "You must be doing a lot of laundry."

I firmly stated, "Just my family's and not the whole neighborhood." I was aware I wasn't helping my case. At this point, my frustration level wasn't functioning at a reasonable level. I couldn't fathom what the bill would be for a full quarter billing cycle! I suspected we were paying the unpaid balance of the last renter's water bill! Regardless, it was a fight I wasn't going to win, so I asked to be put on a payment plan, and they were at least willing to do that.

Not long after the water incident, we were faced with another red flag when I started to notice a gas odor. It seemed to come and go, nothing consistent, but it was disturbing just the same since Terry and his wife Laura both smoked. The kitchen stove was gas-operated so that was the most logical place to check. I had Marc investigate to make sure all the pilot lights were lit and functioning, and the knobs were in the off position. Everything was normal. Terry came upstairs expressing the same concern about a heavy gas odor. The origin of the smell remained a mystery, but I wasn't taking any risks and called the gas company. They immediately sent out a technician. He had a gas detection meter that he used to check around the stove but found nothing that would indicate a leak. Terry mentioned that the odor was strong at times, in the basement area, but the technician found no cause for alarm.

I was still very unsettled about the matter! The tech advised me about making sure the knobs on the stove were in the off position, and then he walked outside. Marc was making small talk with the technician in the front yard as he was preparing to leave. Suddenly, his meter went off signaling a dangerously high level of gas right there in the front yard! "Oh, my, we have an underground gas leak right here in your front yard! It's a good thing I forgot to turn my meter off when I came outside!"

He called for a digging crew to come out right away, and just as suspected, a huge leak was discovered. Whenever Terry and Laura smoked, they would open the basement window to usher out some of the cigarette smoke. The window was ground level and faced the front yard, which allowed the gas smell to enter through the window every time it was opened. It also solved the mystery of the smell coming and going.

After the frightening incident, Terry revealed something significant to me. He said that a few nights prior, he was going to discard one of his lit cigarette butts in a drain in the floor that was located on the same side where the leak was discovered, but then he said something strongly urged me not to do it, so I didn't! I believe without a shadow of a doubt Terry heard the voice of the Lord warning him not to follow through with his intentions. I also believe with just as much conviction that when the technician forgot to turn his meter off, it was God's protective hand at work. If Terry had thrown that lit cigarette butt in the floor drain, I believe it could have caused a massive explosion!

Aren't you glad that God sees the danger even when we are unaware of the peril? There is nothing hidden from His sight! In PSALM 91:3, "HE WILL KEEP YOU SAFE FROM ALL HIDDEN DANGER." I am so thankful that He does. I began to ponder whether or not we had an underground water leak as well!

Marc and I had worked for the marble company for a couple of years now and continually taking steps to restore our credit. Our goal was to save for a down payment to purchase a home. We realized it was going to be difficult to achieve our goal while living in a house that was turning into a money pit, not to mention, a safety concern too! I began to look for a more budget-friendly place. My brother Jerry and his family decided to sell their home and move to Florida near Millie. This moving thing must run in the family! We found a mobile home for rent in the same park where my parents lived. It was much smaller but a lot more budget-friendly. We were willing to temporarily sacrifice the space since it would allow us the two years needed to save for a down payment on our future home.

Mom was thrilled to hear we would be living in the same park. Terry and his family were able to find a home in a nearby town. He continued riding to work with us, which made practical sense. One day as the three of us prepared to leave work for the day, Terry received a call on the company phone from his wife, Laura. I could tell by Terry's facial expression that something was wrong. He hung up the phone and said, "Jerry has had an accident!"

Fear gripped me in an icy choke hold! "What's happened?" I asked.

Terry continued, "He was at work [Jerry worked as an auto mechanic] testing a rebuilt hydraulic he had installed on a boom truck. This type of truck has a long extension arm that allows work-men to work in high areas such as power lines and poles. Instead of testing the reconditioned hydraulic remotely from the ground, Jerry made the mistake of testing it from inside the bucket! He had the arm fully extended seventy feet in the air when the hydraulic failed and came crashing down on pavement! The sound could be heard throughout the industrial park with many people leaving their work-stations to come outside and investigate the loud crashing sound."

When I heard the devastating details, I felt the strength leave my body! *Oh, my God! How can anyone survive such a horrendous fall?* I thought. The situation looked very grave for Jerry. There were no other details to go on other than he was still alive and had been taken to the hospital. I felt sick to my stomach at the thought of possibly losing another brother! My main concern for Jerry was that he didn't know Jesus as his personal Savior.

As the three of us made the long ride home, I began praying desperately, "Lord! Don't let Jerry die! He doesn't know you, Father. Give him another opportunity!" I cried. I began to pray against any brain trauma or any other injury that may threaten his life. I kept repeating that prayer all the way home despite the *What ifs?*

After arriving home, I found Mom was already there waiting by the phone for any word on Jerry's condition. We kept praying as we anticipated the call. The wait was agonizing! After what seemed like an eternity, we received a call from Liz on Jerry's condition. He had a broken jaw, crushed chin, two broken wrists, a broken thumb, but no brain trauma or any other life-threatening injuries! He was going to make it! One of the attending physicians was quoted as saying, "I have seen people fall from forty feet and not live to tell about it, but falling from seventy feet onto concrete is unheard of. It's amazing he has no brain injury!"

I believe that classifies as a miracle! By all outward circumstances, Jerry should have been dead, but God hears our desperate prayers. In Hebrews 13:8, "Jesus Christ is the same yesterday and today and forever." He is still a waymaker and a miracle worker.

Jerry had a long road of recovery ahead of him, but thank God it was better than planning another funeral. Mom and I went down to Florida for a week to help out with Jerry's needs after his hospital release. From the time of his accident to the present, I have never failed to remind my brother that it was a miracle from God that saved his life, a fact he cannot deny!

Just four days following Jerry's accident, our family was in need of another miracle. My brother Eugene and his wife Laura (I have two sisters-in-law with the same name) lived in Washington state. Eugene enjoyed getting together with friends and playing sports. As one growing up with him, I can affirm that Eugene plays aggressively. His wife, Laura, called to inform the family that Eugene was in the hospital undergoing emergency surgery for a perforated spleen.

While playing football with friends, Eugene became injured when he and another player tried catching the football at the same time as they both fell to the ground. The other player landed on Eugene with the force of his elbow going deep into his abdomen, which split his spleen nearly in half! He was bleeding to death internally. The guy who fell on him was twice his size and weight! We covered Eugene in prayer, and the Lord faithfully brought him through the surgery. The surgeon said if Eugene had been five minutes later getting to the hospital, he would have died! Almost losing two of my brothers in less than a week was a bit overwhelming.

Personally, it was a time to exhale and meditate on the goodness of God. The enemy came roaring against my brothers, but Jesus said, "No!" In PSALM 27:13, "I WOULD HAVE LOST HEART UNLESS I HAD BELIEVED THAT I WOULD SEE THE GOODNESS OF THE LORD IN THE LAND OF THE LIVING." Eugene made a full recovery and now spends most of his recreational time hunting. God is so good!

Marc and I established a small cultured marble repair business that we worked on outside of our regular jobs. The extra revenue was helping us attain our desired goal to buy a home. The added work hours could be long and grueling, but we stayed focused on our objective. One cold winter night as we made our way home from a side job, I glanced out my window and noticed something very bizarre. We were traveling on a two-lane back road that at the time was deserted. I looked up at the night sky and clearly saw a cross that was casting a light beam to the ground! *Were my eyes deceiving me?* I thought. I had Marc stop the car since we were the only ones on the road, and I put my window down to be certain that it wasn't a glare coming from the window, but it was still there! I asked Marc to lean over and look up at the sky and said, "What do you see?"

"Wow! That's a cross!"

We were out in the middle of nowhere; there was no logical explanation for what we both were seeing!

I put my window back up and laughed as I told Marc, "You know when we tell others about this, they are never going to believe us!"

Marc said, "You're probably right."

As we began to drive away, Marc noticed a pickup truck that had passed us on the opposite side of the road. We both would find out the meaning of the glowing cross and the truck but not until twenty years later. Let's fast-forward for a moment. Marc and I had gone to bed for the night. I immediately fell asleep, but Marc lay awake praying and asking the Lord if he could witness some type of a miraculous sign. He wasn't asking in order to believe God was real; he was hungry to see more of God's glory on a higher level.

The Lord spoke and said, "I GAVE YOU A SIGN!"

Marc replied, "What sign, Lord?"

Suddenly, in a vision, Marc saw the glowing cross we had both witnessed twenty years before.

Then the Lord spoke again, "I PUT THAT CROSS IN THE SKY TO STOP YOU THAT NIGHT BECAUSE THERE WAS A DRUNK DRIVER IN A TRUCK UP AHEAD THAT HAD CROSSED THE CENTERLINE AND WOULD HAVE HIT YOU HEAD-ON AND KILLED YOU BOTH IF I HADN'T CAUSED YOU TO STOP."

The next morning, Marc was hesitant to tell me what the Lord revealed to him the night before. When we joined hands for our devotional prayer time, I became consumed with the presence of the Holy Spirit and, as is my nature, started to weep. I looked at Marc and said, "I don't know why, but I am feeling the strong presence of the Lord for some reason!"

Marc looked at me and said, "I know why! I wasn't going to tell you, but now I know the Lord wants me to!"

When Marc told me what the Lord revealed to him the night before, I fell to my knees weeping with thankfulness! At that moment, I felt it was impossible to thank the Lord enough. The goodness and love of God engulfed my entire being! Marc and I were clueless our lives were in imminent danger that night. I believe the truck Marc saw passing us was the truck that would have hit us. Satan desired to kill Marc and me, but Jesus gave us his lifesaving cross!

IN PSALM 56:13, "FOR YOU HAVE DELIVERED MY LIFE FROM DEATH, YES, AND MY FEET FROM FALLING, THAT I MAY WALK BEFORE GOD IN THE LIGHT OF LIFE AND OF THE LIVING."

14

God Keeps Calling!

After living in the park for two years, we secured the down payment to purchase a home and were more than ready to move. Moving closer to work was a high priority, so our search began in the southern Maryland area. Marc and I had made that long trip from Laurel to White Plains for over four years, and it was time to shorten the drive! Not to mention, the further south you went, the home prices were more reasonable. Mom was happy for us, but at the same time, she was hoping we would remain in the Laurel area. She had enjoyed the closeness of us living four doors down from her and Dad and the Bible time that she and I had shared.

I signed on with a realtor who found us a home in a suburb called Mechanicsville. Marc and I loved its laid-back country surroundings and the small pockets of Amish farms. We still had a thirty minute drive to work, but compared to the previous drive, it was much shorter. Our two older boys, John and David, stayed in the Laurel area. Being of legal age, that was their choice, and Scott and Bobbie moved with Marc and me.

We moved a couple of days before Christmas. The weather was chilly but abundant with sunshine. All things considered, it was a great moving day! The following weekend after the move, we had a blizzard that dropped eighteen inches of snow. Too close for comfort! Having been a native of Ohio, Marc was accustomed to those kinds of snowstorms, but Maryland rarely saw snowfalls of that magnitude. Like I said earlier, I didn't mind one good snowfall a year.

Marc had a best friend named Homer who he grew up with and who resided in Ohio. They managed to stay in touch over the years. Whenever Homer called, Marc would take the opportunity to witness to him about Christ. Although Homer wasn't open to receiving Jesus as his Savior, he wasn't offended by Marc's witness and would still call every so often to catch up. Then there was an expanse of time where Marc wasn't hearing from Homer, and I said to Marc, "Hasn't it been a while since you've heard from Homer?"

"Yes! Now that you mention it, I need to give him a call," he said.

A short time after that, Marc got a call from Homer's wife, Bobby-Jo, telling him that Homer had died! Marc was shocked and devastated to hear such unexpected news! "What happened?" he asked. She explained through tears that Homer had become very ill with a virus that took his life!

Marc immediately began to reflect on him and Homer's many conversations about the Lord and how his best friend wasn't ready to meet Jesus. Marc was heartbroken! Then, Bobby-Jo revealed something miraculous during the tearful conversation with Marc. She said, "Marc! Homer got saved! A few hours before he died, he asked to speak with a preacher about salvation. Homer said there had to be something to this Jesus and being saved if Marc believed it, so he got saved!" After hearing about the final moments of Homer's life, Marc was overcome with tears of thankfulness for what the Lord had done! Truly the most wonderful miracle of all is receiving Jesus as your Savior.

Marc and I both took away an invaluable lesson from the outcome of his best friend's life, and that was to never underestimate the power of your testimony to others. Just when you think your witness is falling on deaf ears, God is at work on the hidden heart. As Christians, we must be ready in and out of season to share our faith. We are responsible for sowing the seed of the gospel and leaving the effect of that sown seed to God alone! In 1 PETER 3:15, "BUT IN YOUR HEARTS REGARD CHRIST THE LORD AS HOLY, READY AT ANY TIME TO

GIVE A DEFENSE TO ANYONE WHO ASKS YOU FOR A REASON FOR THE HOPE THAT IS IN YOU."

Marc drew tremendous comfort in knowing Homer was not eternally lost but at home in heaven with his Savior.

After getting settled in our new home, I decided to take Samson for a walk and get acquainted with our neighborhood. I was on the walk for about ten minutes when I heard a loud clopping sound approaching from behind. I turned to see an Amish buggy coming my way, and I stopped to get a better look as it drew closer. The horses were massive! Samson's reaction to the horses caught me completely off-guard! He became terrified at the sight of these massive creatures, and without warning, he pulled himself out of his collar and bolted!

I was left standing with a collar and leash in my hand. I had never seen my fearless dog so traumatized, poor Sam! Having no idea where he ran off to, I made my way back home with collar and leash in hand. I was thankful to find Samson waiting by the front door when I got home. He eagerly went inside and found a safe place to lay down.

I found my life had become much busier since moving to Mechanicsville. The company we worked for was booming, and it required Marc and me to work copious amounts of overtime! Coupled with that, our side business was picking up steam as well. We barely had any real quality downtime to enjoy the fruit of our labor.

One of the most important things I neglected to do in all of my busyness was to find a new church home. The real issue was my failure to prioritize! I kept putting it off with the excuse, "I'll get to it later!" I had become caught up in the money we were making and poured myself into my job and working the side business almost every Saturday! I tried convincing myself that I would find a home church and get back on track, but with each passing week, I thought about it less and less until I no longer concerned myself with it.

In HEBREWS 10:25, "AND LET US NOT NEGLECT OUR MEETING TOGETHER, AS SOME PEOPLE DO, BUT ENCOURAGE ONE ANOTHER, ESPECIALLY NOW THAT THE DAY OF HIS RETURN IS DRAWING NEAR."

I had begun a downward spiral and was moving further away from the presence of God. I occasionally had twinges of guilt when I considered the kindness and goodness of God in my life, but I quickly pushed those thoughts aside and refused to park there. Mom was disheartened to learn I was no longer walking in the will of the Lord. I was back on the road called "my will," and I would travel that road for the next ten years; but the Holy Spirit's unfailing love had another future divine setup in store for me that would put me back on the right path and, this time, keep me there!

Marc and I continued to do well on our jobs, and the extra money we took in from our side business was spent on nonessential things we enjoyed and small remodel projects on our new home. Whenever our side business brought us close to the Laurel area, we would stop in to see how my parents were getting along. With Carol living close by, I was thankful that she frequently made welfare checks on them.

In a few years, we sold our home in Mechanicsville and bought a larger residence in White Plains. We now lived within eight minutes of work, and that afforded me the luxury of hitting the snooze button on my alarm a few more times before getting up for work. Another positive about the move was it put us thirty minutes closer to Mom and Dad although the drive was still an hour.

But life for my parents was about to make a sudden drastic change. The park management informed their residents the property had been sold to a developer, and the residents would need to relocate their mobile homes. This was not welcome news for my parents, especially my mother! With Dad living on a fixed income, they couldn't afford to relocate their home. Another issue they faced was their home was an older model, and none of the other parks in the vicinity were willing to take in their aged home. Mom instantly went into a deep depression at the thought of pulling up long-established roots, but it was clear a solution was needed; they had to have help! That help came in the form of an end-of-year-employee bonus Marc and I had just received. The bonuses together would pay to move their home, but I had to locate a park that was willing to take in their dated home.

My search led me to a park that was located in the city of Waldorf, which happened to be eighteen minutes from where Marc and I lived, and it was affordable. Mom was distraught about moving that far from Laurel. I truly understood her deep-seated attachment to the area she had called home for many years, but there was no plan B! I also felt she wasn't showing ample gratitude for our efforts to help her and Dad, and I felt offended. I never expected such a negative reaction from her. I thought the opposite. My father, on the other hand, would acclimate just fine. I moved forward with the hope that, in time, Mom would adjust to her new surroundings, but I would ultimately come to the startling conclusion my hope would never come to fruition.

It grieved me to see her so withdrawn. I almost felt guilty for moving them. Dad was able to relocate his shed in the move, and that alone made him quite happy. He always had the ability to pick up from where he left off once the dust settled. Over recent years, my mother had also developed an addiction to prescription drugs, which only attributed to her depression even more! Whenever I would talk with her on the phone, her voice was devoid of any enthusiasm, almost monotone, which increased my concern about her mental and physical health. At times, I tried talking to her about the medication, but she made it clear that talking about her meds was strictly off-limits!

Dad and I both worked in tandem to try and bring Mom out of her depression. She loved to receive gifts, so I bought things that I knew she liked, and Dad went to work in his shed making her favorite yard ornaments or birdhouses. He even placed a birdbath outside of her bedroom window so she could lay on her bed and watch the birds she dearly loved splash around. Still, there was little to no emotion! I was beginning to lose hope that Mom would ever come out of her depression.

Our boss offered Dad a part-time position, which helped supplement his fixed income. He enjoyed his new position and the new friends he was making with the other workers who affectionately called him pappy. A few years had passed since I had strayed away from the Lord although I often thought about my eternal destiny. These thoughts would rekindle my deep-seated desire to run back to the Lord and tell Him how sorry I was for turning my back on Him and rededicate my life once again, but I was plagued with guilt and shame for turning away from Him!

There was another sinister voice that was always ready to accuse me as well, Satan! He whispered his lie, "Do you really think God would forgive you after all the sinful things you've done? You walked away from Him, and He is not pleased with you! You have gone too deep in your sin this time, and God is very angry with you!" REVELATION 12:10 tells us Satan accuses us before the Lord day and night; he never ceases!

I came into agreement with his lies, which empowered him to work against me. *After all,* I thought, *God had to be angry with me for everything I have done!* This lie made God unapproachable for me when I looked at Him through the filter of my earthly father. Like I said in an earlier chapter, my father stayed angry most of the time, and he never told any of his children that he loved them while growing up! Those roots will follow a child right into adulthood. Satan's destructive lies have been, and still are, effective weapons in his arsenal. I have met many people in my life who have said, "God would never forgive me for the things I have done." That's one of Satan's most effective lies! Like me, if he can keep you in a constant state of guilt and condemnation, then he has succeeded in making you believe you are permanently broken and keeping a wall between you and God!

No sin that you have ever committed can keep you from God's loving forgiveness. You are never too far gone in your sin that He can't hear you when you cry out to Him or heal your broken past! God has been waiting your whole life to hear you call on His name. In 1 John 1:9, "IF WE CONFESS OUR SINS TO HIM, HE IS FAITHFUL AND JUST TO FORGIVE US OUR SINS AND CLEANSE US FROM OUR WICKEDNESS."

At this juncture in my life, I had fallen victim to Satan's lies. I felt so guilty and unworthy that I wouldn't dare to ask God for forgiveness. But it was never about me being worthy; it's about Jesus being worthy! What can wash away my sins? Nothing but the blood of Jesus! Like many times before, I pushed my eternal destiny to a back burner and moved on with my life, that is, until the next time the Holy Spirit lovingly tugged on my heartstrings.

Martha, Martha, Come Sit at My Feet

Martha, Martha, come sit at my feet
Your life is so busy, and your troubles run deep
You fret and you worry about what's not getting done
Slow down for a time, I bid you to come
I call to you often, but my voice goes unheard
Your schedule is so full, there's no time for my word
The burdens you carry have made your shoulders weak
You're so worn out and tired that you fall fast asleep
The morning it dawns, and I have many things to say
But I can't tell you a thing till you slow down and pray
Come to the place where all time stands still
Be silent before me, and I shall tell you my will
The enemy keeps you bound up and stressed
He has stolen your joy till you no longer feel blessed
Come to my well and drink deeply of me
There in my presence, you will have my true peace

In Luke 10:41–42, "Martha, Martha, the Lord replied, you are worried and upset about many things. But only one thing is necessary. Mary has chosen the good portion, and it will not be taken away from her."

15

The Turning Point!

Our son David, met Jennifer, the girl of his dreams, and they were married. They eventually had two children with the youngest being an infant. One day out of the blue, David called to invite Marc and me to our grandson's baby dedication. It was to be held in the Baptist church Jennifer had attended while growing up. When Marc informed me of David's request, I went into a full-blown panic mode! "What! Marc, we haven't been to a church in years!" Here came the unworthiness, condemnation, guilt, shame, and let's not forget about God being angry! All of the lies came at me like flashing neon signs! It wasn't that I didn't want to go; it was I felt too sinfully dirty, if you will, to step inside of God's Holy sanctuary! Clearly, I was still in agreement with the enemy's deceptive lies!

We had to go! It was an invitation we couldn't refuse although Marc wasn't experiencing any of the panic attacks that I was. I had two weeks to prepare, and my anxiety level was off the hook! I was certain the moment I stepped inside that sanctuary, all eyes would be on me and thinking to themselves, *We have a sinner in our midst!* As crazy as that sounds, my fear was very real, nonetheless. Fear is another highly effective weapon in Satan's arsenal that he often uses against us!

In 2 Timothy 1:7, "For God has not given us a spirit of fear, but of power and of love and a sound mind." We can be certain from reading the above verse that fear doesn't come from

God so that leaves the origin to only one culprit! "Fear not" is in the Bible 365 times. That's one "fear not" for every day of the year, and I needed a "fear not" as in yesterday!

But God had a plan for me that Satan couldn't thwart, and it was about to unfold! In Isaiah 55:9, "For as the heavens are higher than the earth, so are my ways higher than your ways and my thoughts higher than your thoughts." As we pulled into the church parking lot, my stomach felt like it was tied in knots! I convinced myself not to make eye contact with anyone other than family. I took one last look in the visor mirror to make sure I didn't have sinner stamped on my forehead and proceeded to the entrance. I glanced over at Marc to see how he was doing, but he didn't seem to be experiencing any of the ill effects I was.

Upon entering the foyer, we were immediately greeted by David and Jennifer, which was a welcome relief. I nervously looked around but didn't notice anyone staring at me suspiciously, and the roof wasn't falling in on me! A few of the church members greeted Marc and me with warm friendly smiles, and my stomach knots started to dissipate one by one. *Maybe it wouldn't be so bad after all,* I thought. *The ceremony would be over before I knew it, and we would be on our way back home.*

We entered the sanctuary and found some seats close to the front. I looked around and noticed how nice the sanctuary was. I finally found myself at ease, thinking, *I've got this!* Within a few minutes, the worship music started. The songs were amazingly beautiful! It had been years since I had heard worship music like this, and it was having an effect on me! The songs ministered straight to my heart! Something deep within me started to stir, something very unexpected! It was beyond goosebumps! *What's going on?* I was suddenly reminded of the Holy Spirit's convicting love I had felt as a teenager many years before in the church revival in Beltsville. It was the same convicting love that was presently washing over my entire being! Holy Spirit in His love and tender mercy was calling me again!

I quickly brushed the tears away before any of my family members noticed. It was a divine setup! *Not now, Lord. I'm not ready!* Then, thankfully, the music stopped, and the pastor stepped forward to begin the baby dedication ceremony. It gave me the much-needed opportunity to get myself under control. It was beautiful to watch these precious babies dedicated back to their maker, but I had my eye on the exit!

After the service, I shared my experience with Marc as we made our way home. I confessed to him that I had no doubt the Lord was calling me back to Him. All my years of living in rebellion and God still lovingly continued to call me. Not once did I feel any anger coming from my Heavenly Father; no, it was quite the opposite! Every fiber of my being felt nothing but His love. Satan is a liar, and he never changes. On the rest of the drive home, I was sensing something deep in the depths of my soul, a powerful knowing if you will that I was on the verge of a significant turning point in my life, but I wasn't able to put my finger on it just yet.

Four years had passed since my parents had moved to Waldorf, and Mom still suffered from bouts of depression. She occasionally had moments where the sun broke through the clouds, but I could always sense that she wasn't happy. Every time I spoke with her whether on the phone or in person, the depression seemed to hang in the air like a heavy curtain. It continued to grieve me to see her that unhappy.

One afternoon, Mom called, and Marc answered the phone. After exchanging a few words with Mom, Marc handed me the receiver and whispered, "Your mother sounds really good, Sue!" His statement made my heart leap with hope and joy!

Maybe she is finally turning that emotional corner out of her depression I thought as I took the phone. "Hello, Mom." I was astonished at how much joy and clarity I heard in her voice! Marc wasn't exaggerating in the least bit. It had been years since I had heard her speak with such enthusiasm. My heart was doing somersaults! I have my mother back, yes! During our conversation, I had a strong impression to share my experience with her that I had at the church two weeks prior.

Mom quietly listened as I relayed every detail. "Mom, I have to confess that the conviction of the Lord's love consumed me. I believe He is calling me back to Him."

Then my mother responded, "Susie, the Lord has called you to be a minister, and I have known this for many years, but you have chosen your own path in life."

As Mom spoke those words to me, I felt the stirring of the Holy Spirit in my heart, and tears began welling up in my eyes. There was a heaviness to her words that I couldn't explain. They were piercing my heart! Why were her words impacting? I was finding it difficult to keep my composure. She continued by saying, "The Lord is still calling you."

I said, "Mom, if that's the case, I'm asking the Lord to open that door for me."

She replied, "Susie, He will!" Little did I realize at that moment, as God opened that door for me, another would soon be closing!

After hanging up the phone, I told Marc how deeply touching the conversation had been and how lucid Mom was. I was holding onto hope that she was transitioning for the better. As it turned out, my mother did make a transition, but it wasn't at all what I had expected. My life was on the threshold of a major turn, one I could now put my finger on. That special conversation was the last one I would share with my mother, on this earth. Four days later, she died!

16

And the Birds Still Sing

As Marc and I continued making our way to the park where my parents lived, I began thinking about how quickly my thoughts about Mom changed from the present tense to the past tense. I wasn't prepared for her unexpected departure with so many words left unsaid, words that had now become invaluable. I didn't get to say goodbye or tell her how much I loved her one last time! I wanted to thank her for teaching me about Jesus, oh, how my heart ached! I felt like a small child who was lost and couldn't find her mother.

We arrived at my parents just as a police officer was exiting the front door and preparing to leave. At my insistence, I had Marc approach the officer and ask if my mother's body had been removed. The officer confirmed that the coroner had just left with her body. I couldn't emotionally handle knowing that my mom was still inside. I found Dad sitting alone on the couch and sobbing as we entered their home. His brokenness reminded me of the day he discovered my brother's lifeless body years earlier! I quickly ran over to him and wrapped my arms around him. He looked at me with such sorrowful tear-filled eyes and said, "She's gone!"

"Dad, what happened?"

He began, "Hours earlier, I went into her room to check on her, and she began to thank me for always taking care of her, and she said, 'I'm going to leave now!' It really upset me to hear her talking like that, and I told her I didn't want to hear that kind of talk, but she repeated it a second time!

"That's when I got angry and left the room."

In truth, I knew Dad was fearful due to the implications of what Mom was trying to tell him, and that was goodbye! In the early hours before dawn, he went back in to check on Mom only to find that she had passed! He wasn't ready to let her go, and neither was I. We couldn't stay long because other family members were already on the way to our home. Not wanting my father to be alone, I asked him if he wanted to come back to the house with us, but he declined and said he preferred to stay there at home for a while. I didn't want to leave him at such a vulnerable time, but I respected his wishes. I felt such sorrow for my father, knowing this was the second time he had found a deceased family member.

When Marc and I got in the car and drove away, I began to reflect on my conversation with Mom days earlier. The extraordinary clarity and joy in her voice, emotions I hadn't heard from her in years! How spiritually impactful her words had been and how much they affected me. I was becoming more persuaded by the minute that my last conversation with my mother was a divine appointment! The very woman who prayed a fervent prayer for her lost fourteen-year-old daughter's soul was the very same woman the Holy Spirit used to get her daughter back on the narrow way once again!

It all made sense to me now! Mom gave me Holy Spirit-inspired instructions before departing this earth!

Not long after arriving home, family members began showing up. The grieving process was in full gear, but like my father, I needed to be alone for a time. What I truly desired was time to be alone with the Lord. I had a very heavy heart with a burning question in my soul that I needed the Lord to answer. I told Marc I was going for a walk and left. Although I knew Mom loved the Lord with all of her heart, I still yearned to know from Him if she made it! Was she there in heaven with Him? That may seem like an unnecessary question given her love for the Lord, but I had to know with certainty. I cried out from the depths of my soul as everything else around me faded on my walk, but I heard nothing but the birds singing on this beautiful May morning. I cried out again and again, still nothing!

I returned from my walk discouraged and dejected! Millie began the necessary process of planning the funeral. I was very thankful she took control in such a chaotic time. I was at a loss, wondering how to deal with this huge gaping hole in my life that Mom used to occupy. Nothing could replace her absence. I never could have imagined it would hurt this much! Evening came, and family members left for home. Millie and her family stayed with Marc and me. I was exhausted when bedtime approached, but I felt guilty at the thought of contemplating sleep! *Help me get through this, Lord!* Exhaustion eventually won the battle over my guilt, and I fell asleep.

I awoke the next morning to bright rays of sunshine streaming through the bedroom window. My first agonizing thought was, *Mom is gone! How dare this day be so beautiful. My mother is dead! It should be gloomy and rainy outside. That would have been more fitting, but the weather wasn't cooperating!* I defiantly resolved to stay in bed and have zero participation in this beautiful day. I no sooner made that decision when I suddenly heard a little bird start to sing loudly outside on the window ledge. Because my window was open, the singing was especially loud, and the bird wasn't stopping! *What is going on?* I thought. First, the weather is uncooperative, now a bird bursting at the seams in a joyful song! "Go someplace else and sing your song," and I pulled the blanket over my head.

It was then I heard the gentle voice I had sought so desperately the day before on my walk. "Get up! She's home with the King!" There was no mistaking His voice! I sat bolt upright in bed.

"You have her! He has her! She's home! Thank you, Lord. Thank you!" I was overwhelmed with joy as tears streamed down my face. "God, you are so loving and merciful!" Though I felt all alone on my walk the day before, God was there with me the whole time confirming His promise in Hebrews 13:5, "I will never leave, you nor forsake you."

I took the Holy Spirit's comforting words and hid them deep within my heart. There was still a grieving season to go through, but the Lord's words began the healing process. In the weeks and months ahead, God continued to use His songbirds as a gentle reminder of where my mother was when I had moments of intense grief. Like clockwork, whenever I found myself grieving, a songbird would show up just outside near a window of the room I was in and start to sing. It was as if they were singing into a microphone! It happened so often that Marc was amazed at the timing of these little ones, or should I say the Lord's.

Once, when I was younger, my mother shared a dream with me. She dreamed of being in heaven, about how beautiful and indescribably peacefilled it was. When she awoke from the dream and realized that she was no longer in heaven, she was extremely disappointed. The experience for Mom was very real. In her words, "I wanted to stay!" Her wish to stay had been fulfilled. It was now God's turn to celebrate the passing of one of His children who has eternally entered His kingdom.

In PSALM 116:15, "PRECIOUS IN THE SIGHT OF THE LORD IS THE DEATH OF HIS FAITHFUL SERVANTS." Mom is very much alive right now as I pen these words. She is beholding the face of her beloved Savior. It grieves my heart to let go of her for a little while, but as David said of his deceased son in 2 SAMUEL 12:23, "I WILL GO TO HIM, BUT HE SHALL NOT RETURN TO ME." David knew he would one day see his child again when he entered heaven.

I continually stand in awe of God's loving mercy and His mysterious ways! How He used His creation, the tiny birds that my mother dearly loved, to speak joy, comfort, and peace at the perfect moments in my life!

At the beginning of this book, you read a poem about the choir of birds. God speaks to us in many ways, and He still uses these little ones to let us know in PSALM 30:5, "WEEPING MAY ENDURE FOR A NIGHT, BUT JOY COMES IN THE MORNING." This verse was fulfilled in my life on May 10, 2005! I have a bird feeder just outside my living room window where I have a front-row seat to watch the birds come and go, especially Mom's favorite, the cardinal. They are constant reminders that though there are storms and trials, the birds still sing! HALLELUJAH!

In Psalm 84:3, "Even the sparrow has found a home, and the swallow a nest for herself, where she may have her young, a place near your altar, Lord Almighty, my King and my God!"

The Invitation

My child, do not be fearful of what your eyes may see.
Just live among the branches and stay connected to the tree.
For I am still the "Tree of Life". Hear my voice both loud and strong,
Just know I'm waiting for you to join their song.
So send your voices toward the sky, raise your hands, lift them high!
In praise and worship to the King. Oh, let the hallelujah ring!
I am Jesus, Savior, and Lord.
I will keep my promises and honor my word.
Come unto me, and you will find rest.
When I died on the cross, I gave you my best!
Come all who will, and you shall see!
Take my yoke upon you and learn of me!

IN MATTHEW 11:28–30, "COME TO ME, ALL YOU WHO ARE WEARY AND BURDENED, AND I WILL GIVE YOU REST. TAKE MY YOKE UPON YOU AND LEARN FROM ME, FOR I AM GENTLE AND HUMBLE IN HEART, AND YOU WILL FIND REST FOR YOUR SOULS. FOR MY YOKE IS EASY AND MY BURDEN IS LIGHT."